LEADING
WITH YOUR
HEAD
AND YOUR
HEART

Creating Organizational Culture
to Yield Extraordinary Business Results

WILLIAM C. LUCIA
WITH DEBORAH KELLY

This book is dedicated to the HMS workforce, past and present. Without your passion, urgency and heart, none of these amazing results would have been possible.

Contents

Foreword by
Dr. John Kotter

I've spent the many decades of my career fascinated by organizations that are able to perform exceptionally well by, essentially, beating the odds when it comes to change. In the mid-90s, I wrote an article all about "why transformation efforts fail", which they do all the time. The research upon which that piece was based has subsequently guided my own work and framed my firm's work for the last dozen-or-so years.

So, when I uncover success stories, I tend to pay attention. And I start asking questions… What led to the success? As our understanding of change continues to evolve, what can we learn?

Much of what we have learned as a firm (Kotter International) has been through our partnerships with organizations undergoing transformational change. We bring our deep expertise, and our clients bring their specific challenges and opportunities in the context of their situation and their culture. In the best of scenarios, our relationship is truly symbiotic.

HMS is a shining example of this.

What I observed in the five years we worked alongside HMS was an executive team that was committed to achieving their opportunity, and an organization that was dedicated to becoming students of change. Bill and his team were not afraid to challenge me and my team when the journey felt hard – and we were bold in pushing them to the far edges of their comfort zone.

HMS put into practice what we have recently articulated as the Science of Change: an awareness of our human response to change; the benefits and limitations of a traditional organizational hierarchy; and the framework and principles for leading change that have proven successful since the emergence of the modern organization.

As you will soon learn in reading this manuscript, Bill and Deb (and many, many others on Bill's team) have much to be proud of as they look to the legacy they built at HMS.

Dr. John Kotter
Konosuke Matsushita Professor of Leadership Emeritus,
Harvard Business School
Co-Founder and Executive Chairman, Kotter International

 Regarded by many as the authority on leadership and change, John P. Kotter is a New York Times best-selling author, award winning business and management thought leader, business entrepreneur, inspirational speaker and Harvard Professor. His ideas, books, speeches, and company, Kotter International, have helped mobilize people around the world to better lead organizations, and their own lives, in an era of increasingly rapid change.

Introduction

I had the honor to serve as Chairman, President, and Chief Executive Officer of HMS—which was a leading healthcare analytics and technology company—for 12 years. I started working at HMS in 1996 and was promoted to CEO in 2009. Finally, I was named Chairman of the Board of Directors in July of 2015.

HMS Holdings (HMSY) Stock Chart 1999-2021

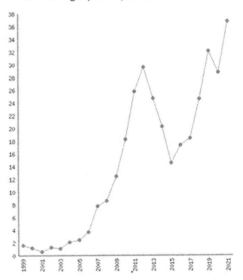

In achieving this level of success, I beat the odds. According to Statista, fewer than 1% of working Americans become CEO. Online Casino's article "The Odds of Success" asserts that even those who hold an MBA have only a 1 in 135,000 chance of becoming CEO. And I don't have an MBA.[1]

---

[1] OnlineCasino.ca. "The Odds of Success: Betting on Fame and Fortune." (n.d.). https://www.onlinecasino.ca/odds-of-success/.

But even after achieving this status, the path is not easy. You still must succeed. The average tenure for a CEO is 4.9 years. The turnover rate is about 16.5%. But I was with HMS for 25 years and served as its leader for over 12. During that time, we were able to deliver impressive results by serving our customers and creating value for our shareholders. [2]

It wasn't always easy. HMS was not always a thriving enterprise. Like any company, we had our twists and turns. We were on a rather slippery slope in 2001, when our stock price plummeted to $57 cents a share and we faced being de-listed from NASDAQ. While I'm glad those dark days are in my rear-view mirror, they also served as a reminder to avoid the mistakes that got us to that point.

At that stage in my career, I was part of an executive team challenged by our Board of Directors to turn the company around. We owned several un-integrated businesses from acquisitions, suffered from negative cash flow, and had no clear strategy for where we were headed.

It took years—and several executive teams—to peel off the businesses that didn't fit with our strategy and for the company to grow again, both organically and through acquisition. But we did. From 2014–2020, we saw a 53% increase in revenue, an 82% jump in Adjusted Earnings Before Interest, Taxes, Depreciation and Amortization (AEBITDA), and a significant stock price surge, all while retaining 97% of top talent and a 91% Glassdoor CEO approval rating by the end of that journey. Our employee engagement scores in that same time frame soared from 61.7% to 82.8%. Employees rated manager effectiveness at 89%. When we were sold to Veritas Capital in 2021 at a valuation of $3.4 billion dollars, we had a stock price of $37.00 per share.

How did I pull all that off?

While I am proud of my intellect, I often didn't view myself as the smartest guy in the room. Nor did I fit the old stereotype of the ruthless

---

[2] https://maexecsearch.com/average-c-suite-tenure-and-other-important-executive-facts

Leading with Your Head and Your Heart

"win at all costs" executive. I understood boardroom politics, but I didn't partake in them. I could be logical and analytical. I was an effective manager in that I could translate my vision to a roadmap that people could follow and execute. I was always able to direct the day-to-day work efforts of staff and anticipate and respond to their needs. I could effectively establish work rules, processes, standards, and operating procedures, and I achieved results through people. But it wasn't just that.

I used my head, but I also used my heart. And that, I believe, is how I did it. This book is about the leadership journey—and the cultural journey—that I have taken my entire career. I hope my story will give you a new perspective of what's possible, and perhaps give you some new skills to enhance your ability to lead—and succeed alongside— your employees through fast-changing environments.

I'll say something controversial: if you lead with just your head, you may gain short-term results, but you will not have an army of engaged employees ready to knock it out of the park for the long-term. We're all humans with heads and hearts, and we typically spend more waking hours at work (or thinking about work) than we do with our own loved ones. So, why not engage the hearts of your workforce so they can surpass your expectations because they *want to* and not because they feel they *must*?

I have always believed passionately in the value of HMS's work. The United States spends $4 Trillion dollars annually on healthcare, an amount that increases every year. While the US spends more on healthcare than any other high-income country, we have worse outcomes: the largest chronic disease burden, the most hospitalizations from preventable causes, and the highest rate of avoidable deaths. Our healthcare system still suffers from huge gaps in quality and access for many and improving health equity remains a challenge in the United States. As a publicly traded (NASDAQ) healthcare information technology company, our mission was to make the healthcare system better for everyone. Throughout our history, we served our nation's safety net healthcare programs through hospitals, Medicaid agencies, and our national Medicare program, and we helped to keep health care accessible by working with health plans and insurers. By the time I left the company, we were recovering over $3 billion dollars a year for our clients and saving them an additional $6 billion per year in costs avoided.

We were also engaging with nearly one million patients a day to help them be better healthcare consumers, remind them to get necessary services, and improve their quality of life and the outcomes achieved from the services they received.

That's a lot of big numbers, huh? Tremendous results, sure. But just the tip of the iceberg in stabilizing a health care system with costs spiraling out of control.

That is the contribution the people at HMS became deeply passionate about; but I'd argue that you can accomplish our level of success with any company, large or small, no matter your industry. What is the value you are creating for your customers and shareholders? What social good are you fostering in the communities where you live and work? What purpose do you serve beyond the acquisition of wealth for your shareholders? Why should your workforce care? And how can you invite them all to play a meaningful role in driving the success of your mission toward that greater good? In this book, we outline how we did it and illustrate how to apply the same concepts to your business.

At the heart of any great company are great people. We didn't do this alone. Throughout the book, we will reference other experts and books that helped us along our journey. Special thanks go to Dr. John Kotter and the team at Kotter Inc. and Debjani Biswas from Coachieve LLC, who were by our sides every step of the way.

This book is for leaders—and those who aspire to lead. It is a story about my career journey, and it is a labor of love. It is a tribute to the entire HMS workforce who helped to create and sustain such astonishing results. And it is a roadmap to help you do the same with your own company and on your own career journey.

Why It Matters

There was a painting that hung just outside my office, across from our executive boardroom. It was the only painting HMS ever commissioned. It's called "Hope" and was painted by Kristan Five (https://kristanfive.com/), the daughter of an employee. I described my vision of what the company's mission meant to me, and the artist portrayed that vision brilliantly. The plaque beside it reads:

> *"In this jewel-like abstract painting, Hope is represented through the thick and intense brushstrokes of an illuminating sun. The figures below it suggests people—arms and faces uplifted toward the promise of something better. For HMS, this promise includes a more cost-effective healthcare system that provides quality coverage for more of our citizens and their families—advancing them to a more secure future. HMS strives to achieve this through service, innovation, excellence and integrity."*
>
> *Bill Lucia, CEO & President, HMS*

This painting means the world to me, and the artist's execution far exceeded my expectations. It symbolizes all my hopes for this company and the difference I believe we can make in the lives of others.

The painting was completed in 2011, and after 10 years, I admit that I barely noticed it most of the time. My days were filled with meetings—with customers, employees, legislators, investors—and all the important activity required to run a Fortune 100 company. But some days, it stopped me. I stood there and reflected or shared the story of the painting's origins with someone else. And I was reminded during those moments of why I joined this great company and have been so proud to lead it.

I joined HMS after having successfully climbed through the executive ranks in a variety of positions in the life insurance industry. I believed in the value of the work I put in with each of those companies. Insurance is important, and people deserve to be protected against loss and financially prepare for their future. Yet I found myself longing to do something that created greater social value—something that would really touch many people's lives, particularly those less fortunate than many of us.

HMS turned out to be the perfect fit. Our company's mission has been to "Make Healthcare Better for Everyone." Through our industry-leading technology, analytics, and engagement solutions, we saved billions of healthcare dollars annually while helping people lead healthier lives. Our broad range of data-intensive, analytical solutions moved healthcare forward by helping healthcare organizations reduce costs and improve health outcomes. We ensured the right bills were paid by the right health insurance payer at the right time. We helped root out fraud, waste, and abuse in the healthcare industry. We provided solutions to engage Americans in their own healthcare. Not only did our work save taxpayer dollars, it also allowed the government to redirect recovered monies to provide healthcare to even more people.

This work was deeply satisfying. With the company's roots serving Medicaid—a health insurance program jointly funded by the states and federal governments—I was able to focus on helping those less fortunate, something I'd been taught to prioritize since an early age. This work filled my soul. Medicaid covers the low-income population, single moms and their children, and disabled individuals. I think of the single mother who can vaccinate her children because of the value we created; the senior who can get a ride to the doctor; and the cancer patient whose life was saved because they acted on our reminder to receive preventive care. These things matter. In a nation filled with health inequities across low-income populations and people of color, our hard work meant more people would not have to choose between receiving much needed medicine or putting food on the table. While I've left this work at HMS in the hands of capable people, it will forever be a dream of mine—and my hope for this country. And I continue to work with companies that can help achieve this dream.

So, helping others became my life's work. I led the company's growth with great pride, but also with great humility, because I have learned throughout my career that no one person can create a great company. It takes every employee—all deeply committed to the company and its mission—to create greatness. Perhaps the ultimate job of a leader is to create an environment that allows the workforce to flourish and gives them the freedom to create greatness. Within this environment, magic happens.

As I began to contemplate the end of my career at HMS, I found myself thinking more and more about everything I learned. From those reflections, this book emerged. As proud as I am of HMS, my truest professional legacy is not the company. Instead, it's the culture that I created in that company—a culture that engages and empowers the workforce, allows them to stretch, experiment, and grow in pursuit of greatness, and that yield results beyond imagination.

Culture matters. Leadership matters. This is the story I want to tell. What we accomplished at HMS is somewhat unique and incredibly special. I believe it can be replicated across many industries and companies. I did not do it alone—no one does. This is the story of how we created a culture that generated results, surpassed all our expectations, and made HMS an ideal place to work. This is a story about leading from the heart.

In the Beginning

Is leadership born or bred? Research suggests both answers are true. As I consider my career, I realize there are traits and values I took from my childhood and others that I learned along the way. Let's start at the beginning.

 I was the third and final child born into a lower middle-class family. I was the "whoops" baby, my mother informed me. My older brother and sister were each a handful in their own way, and my parents hadn't planned on a third. Yet there I was!

My early years were as complicated as anyone else's. My parents were the children of Italian immigrants who grew up during the Depression, and their values reflected that. Mom and Dad were smart and practical people who were denied education and opportunity because they dropped out of high school to help support their families. They met at a textile mill, which were very prevalent in the Northeast at the time (I'm originally from Philadelphia). As I grew up, Mom worked outside the home cleaning doctors' offices, and Dad worked his way up to become a foreman in the textile mill. They shared a once-in-a-lifetime sort of love. They were together for over 70 years and celebrated 69 years of marriage before my mom passed away.

As much as I loved my mother, she was a dichotomy. She could be very warm and loving, and she was a consummate caretaker of both people and animals. Yet she could also be cold and harsh, especially with me as a young child. I suspect she may have suffered with a hidden depression that triggered some of her darker episodes. Whatever the cause, it left me off-balance and anxious for much of my childhood. It also contributed to diminished self-esteem and self-worth, with which I have struggled my whole life. Despite this, I think of my mother every day and I am grateful to be filled with the memories of a smart and funny woman who truly cared for all living beings.

Dad, on the other hand, was a constant stable influence. He was a quiet and contemplative man who wasn't afraid to show his vulnerability.

Leading with Your Head and Your Heart

He wasn't ashamed to wipe tears from his eyes watching an episode of "Lassie" or to give his young son a hug. I remember watching him in the evenings after he'd come home from a full day of work. He would sit with a sheet of graph paper and painstakingly create designs that would end up on the sweaters his mill produced. No one told him to do this, and he wasn't paid for the time he spent on it. He did it because it brought him pleasure. And he was proud of the work he produced. That always stuck with me.

My parents also taught me to work hard, take care of others and know that there are millions of people less fortunate than us. Not that I remember needing anything – I was loved, we were always well-fed, and being the youngest of three children gave me a different perspective than my older brother and sister. My mother's constant reminder that "there are starving children in the world who would want to eat that dinner" wasn't just a way to get us to finish our meal. It was her true devotion, through her faith, to teach her children to be kind to others, and reminding us of the plight of Italians when they emigrated to the U.S. I believe this is why I was so drawn to becoming active in immigration rights later in my life.

I was a chubby kid (I did say we were well fed)with little athletic prowess. I also had a secret, although I wasn't sure how to put it into words at that age. Luckily, I also had a best friend whom I'd met and grown close to in the playpen when we were both toddlers. My friendship with Ricky never waned, even as he grew to become a hero on the football field. People didn't mess with me because no one wanted to mess with him. Tragically, Ricky was struck by a car while trying to cross the street. He was killed when we were in 7th grade.

This was a pivotal point in my development. I was devastated. Mom jumped in to take care of Ricky's larger family—who were obviously shattered at the loss of their brother and son—and she spent all her spare time nurturing them through their grief. It seemed to me that she dismissed my sadness at losing my best friend. She admonished me, reminding me that I was lucky to be alive and that it was Ricky's family that needed all our attention. In retrospect, I realize this may have been her way of dealing with her own heartache. Still, it left me feeling abandoned, by both of them, at a critical time in my development.

What saved me during that time, I believe, was the program I was in at school. I may not have been a star on the athletic field, but I was a bright kid and a National Honor Society scholar. In the sixth grade, a year before I lost my best friend, I was enrolled in an accelerated program that brought together a diverse group of students. Together, we did scholastic work that was a full grade level ahead of our peer group. And in our spare time, we worked with the school's special needs children. The students in this accelerated program were comprised of all the social groups that often segregate in most schools, which brought us together in ways that would not have been possible otherwise. As a result, I built a solid group of diverse friends to lean on after I'd lost Ricky.

In the summer between my freshman and sophomore years of school, I learned to reinvent myself—something I would do again from time to time throughout my life. I grew a little, worked out, and blossomed out of being that chubby kid. I also could suddenly articulate the secret I had been vaguely aware of for most of my life. I knew why I had not experienced the same raging intensity that most of my male friends were experiencing for any of my girlfriends. Even today, with all the societal growth we have seen, it's not easy to come out as gay. It was even harder in the early 1970s. In fact, coming out to my own parents was not a decision I made. Instead, I was "outed" by a friend. Mom cried because I hadn't told them myself, and Dad simply said, "You're my son and I love you." My parents were devout Roman Catholics. But they interpreted their faith's teachings in their own way, which allowed them to accept my truth with grace and love. I will forever be grateful to them for never making me feel guilty of who I am. For this reason, diversity and tolerance became important to me at a young age, and I made sure it was a centerpiece to HMS' culture.

So, what do my beginnings have to do with leadership? As I reflect on my life and my career, I cannot deny that much of what made me successful stemmed from the lessons of my early life.

From my mother, I learned empathy and caretaking, practicality, and self-reliance. From my father, I learned to be disciplined, reflective, intellectually curious, and accepting. From both, I gained a strong work ethic, a big heart, the belief in the need to give back, and a desire to make something of myself. From my best friend, I learned to watch out for the little guy. And from my school friends, I learned the value of bringing together a diverse group of people and encouraging them to excel. Each of those lessons would prove to serve me well throughout my career.

I'll always remember this quote from Pablo Picasso: "The meaning of life is to find your gift. The purpose of life is to give it away." I genuinely believe that when you have a heart ready to serve, you will find a way to use your resources and gifts to help others.

My Career Journey

B ecause of my placement in the accelerated program in high school, I had the option to graduate a year early if I was willing to double up on physical education. Phys Ed twice a day? No thank you. Remember, my intellectual capability far outmatched my athletic ability. So, I chose to stay and graduate with my peers.

For a variety of reasons, I decided to move from high school right into the workforce. Skipping college made sense to 18-year-old me, but if I had a do-over, I would choose otherwise.

It worked for me, though. In the 1970s, there was a much more merit-based system. Hard work and great results could overcome the lack of a degree. I also had inherited my father's intense intellectual curiosity, which drove me to quickly and deeply learn the intricacies of the businesses in which I worked. In today's world, it is much harder to even get the *chance* to prove your ability without a degree. Lack of formal education also adds a degree of insecurity, particularly as you move up the corporate ladder and begin to compete with colleagues who have far more traditional credentials. So, I wouldn't encourage you to take the path I took—but as I said, it worked for me. I never imagined leading teams of PhDs or becoming the CEO of a public company, but I did.

When I was 18, my first job was in the insurance industry with one of the giant companies. I was only one person amongst a sea of desks, but I proudly performed my role as a Clerical Assistant and made $69 a week. As I learned my craft, I was lucky to be hired into a more senior clerical role by a mid-sized life insurance company. That was the start of my rapid career ascension in that industry. Over the next few years, I learned more about the business, moved around the company, and was regularly promoted. I was willing to go wherever they needed me and was transferred in between Philadelphia, San Francisco, and Dallas a few times. Before long, I became the company's youngest Vice President.

I often told this story to people at HMS, primarily to show them that anyone can get anywhere and that I truly understood the challenges of doing their jobs. It made me accessible, and people throughout the company could relate to "someone like them."

Looking back, I can attribute my career success to several things. There were the early lessons that came from growing up in my family and in that specific era. I was blessed with learning agility and an uncanny ability to see and make connections across the business. That allowed me to simplify certain complexities for both myself and others. I had an innate passion for technology, which led me to become an early adopter of new systems and processes—which always gives one an edge over those who resist change.

I remember giving insurance industry presentations on Business Process Reengineering (BPR). I was self-taught using a process that Masaaki Imai, a Japanese organizational theorist and a management consultant of ours, would later name "Kaizen events." (Honestly, I thought I invented it!) I used logic to map out every step in a business process flow and ask these questions:

1. Is this step adding value to the business?
2. Is this step adding value for the customer?
3. Does this step increase cost?
4. Can this step be automated?

BPR was truly my passion in the early days of my career, and I loved to do BPR events with my teams. I would place large sheets of white paper across all the walls in the department so employees could physically participate in asking and answering questions. There's something magical about watching an employee rise from his or her cubicle and start writing comments on a process flow.

I also remember putting up a poster of a cow with a big X through it, which meant "There are no sacred cows." The phrase "because we always did it this way" was not acceptable. This was in the '80s, and these practices—while advanced by more scholarly folks than I—were just part of how I did my job. Naturally, I taught other leaders to do the same. This illustrates how early I adopted the practice of engaging employees in making the business more successful. It is fascinating to look back now and see how these early practices influenced my future.

I was good at measuring outcomes and operational metrics. But I mostly chose leadership over management, and that may have proven to be my most important lesson.

Leadership is not about power, and it never should be. If you believe it is, I'm sorry to say that I don't think you will ever be an outstanding leader unless you change your mindset. Nor do you want to confuse leadership and management. While both are crucial, they are not the same, as we will discuss in detail later.

Management consists of controlling a group or a set of entities to accomplish a goal. Leadership refers to an individual's ability to influence, motivate, and enable others to contribute toward organizational success. Influence and inspiration separate leaders from managers, not power and control.[3]

I began leading people as a young man. I will never forget one particularly memorable employee I hired early in my career at Philadelphia Life Insurance Company. She was brash, outspoken, and not fully qualified for the job she sought. I hired her not for her skillset, but because I saw something in her. She was irreverent and affectionately called me "Baby Boss." Over time, I watched her grow and develop and excel in her job. Not only did she succeed at that job, but I subsequently rehired her when I opened a life insurance underwriting office in Philadelphia for North American Company for Life and Health. Years later, she went on to obtain a PhD in nursing. Talk about making a difference! She taught me a lot: Don't hire just for skills., hire for heart; It's not just about results, it's about people; Care as much about people as you do about results, and the results will come.

During my early years, I realized the people I led weren't as willing to do what I said just because I said so. I had to get them to *want* to do what needed to be done. That took trial and error, but I had several positives on my side. I always cared about the mission of the work I did. I was vocal about the value we created. I cared about the people.

---

[3] HBR.org In Praise of Followers, by Robert Kelley

I think work is fun and winning is fun. And most people like to have fun and like to win! Who doesn't desire a workplace where their ideas are welcomed? Where they can feel confident that everyone is treated equally? That's the environment I sought to create from the beginning of my career.

As my career progressed, I reached a place where people would do what I said just because I said it—even if they disagreed or thought my decisions were the wrong course of action. I will always be glad that my early professional experiences drove me to create an environment of inclusion, where I could be open to discussion and dissent and where, for the most part, people were willing to provide it. Doing so provided the benefit of a diversity of ideas and perspectives. My staff was empowered, meaning that when we agreed on a course of action, people were committed to it. As I became wiser, I learned to listen more generously and show a genuine interest in other points of view. Results invariably improved.

Of course, that doesn't mean there weren't times when I had to make decisions on my own based purely on available data and "gut instinct." That is the job of a CEO. Doing this well is another key executive competency. I call it "logic-based intuition" which entails the ability to integrate logical reasoning effectively and quickly with intuition to drive actions. It means one can make effective "snap judgements" based on an extensive body of experience while also balancing rational and emotional insights into the decision-making process. It also requires that one can effectively explain the rationale behind intuitive decisions so people can get behind those decisions. This is critical—people must understand why they are following or even leading in the directions you've steered them.

That ability led to another critical leadership characteristic—the ability to create followership. After all, one cannot lead if others are not willing to follow. And I believe that you learn to build followership by first *becoming* an effective follower. This does not mean blindly taking orders and executing those orders without thought. In his 1988 HBR article, professor and author Robert Kelley defines the quality of followers:

1. They manage themselves well.
2. They are committed to the organization and to a purpose, principle, or person outside themselves.
3. They build their competence and focus their efforts for maximum impact.
4. They are courageous, honest, and credible.

These are traits I established to manage my own career, and they became the qualities I most valued in the people I surrounded myself with as my career progressed. I can't say that I did this with any grand plan or deep knowledge of the psychology behind leadership or followership. It simply made sense to me to interact with both those above and below me as equals, where we were each committed to a shared purpose, to playing our roles for maximum impact, and to serving our customers to the best of our ability. That it paid off in such a big way was a happy accident. It has been my great joy to build strong teams, many of whom went on to do great things in HMS and other organizations, and some of whom stayed with me as I moved on to new roles and new organizations.

The other characteristic of a great leader is inspiration. People want to know you have a plan—an *exciting* plan—and that they are part of it. Inspiring them to help build the plan and then take the journey is quite different from just telling them, "Here's where we're headed—follow me."

Perhaps the most important thing I learned as I built my career is this: Success should not be a happy accident like it was for me in my early career. Creating the environment that allows people to perform at the highest levels, with joy and pride, should not be left to chance. Organizational cultures that nourish and reward those qualities should be established. So, I came to believe that culture matters more than anything! Without a strong culture, strategy fails. They are inextricably linked.

Building Purposeful Culture

Organizational culture can be defined as the attitudes, beliefs, customs, rituals, and values shared by a community of people which cause those people to behave in specific ways. Every group of people who congregate together has a culture, be it an entire region or country, or a smaller community of people such as a town, a church group, or even a family unit. And of course, every organization has its own culture. Put simply, organizational culture means "how we do things around here."

Left unchecked, a culture will evolve on its own. But I learned through years of working that it is much more effective if one takes a purposeful approach to creating a culture. So, once I was positioned to drive culture, I set out to do so at HMS.

We initially didn't think much about culture. In the beginning, HMS was a small, dynamic, entrepreneurial company. Headquartered in New York City, the team was completely connected. We were united in our mission, and the communication was constant—both formally and on the fly. Due to our niche, there was little credible competition; we would craft unique solutions to serve the individual needs of our customers. We were growing, and we were making money.

Until we weren't.

As we grew, informal communication became more difficult. We began to deploy people across the country. Competition crept in. The customized solutions we were creating for our customers became expensive and difficult to manage. Clearly, we had to change if we wanted to thrive as we had in those early years.

By that time, I had ascended to the role of President and CEO and we had moved our headquarters from New York City to Irving, Texas. The timing was perfect—I could begin to build the purposeful, high-performance culture I instinctively knew would position us for growth. I was committed to bringing forward the entrepreneurial spirit of the old culture while simultaneously building a more employee-centric culture that would fuel our growth.

One of the smartest things I did at the start of this effort was bring in a talented new leader to manage our Human Resources function. Tracy South came with a wealth of experience in human resources and deep expertise in leading organizational change. During the nearly nine years we worked together, Tracy became a confidant, coach, and trusted colleague. Unlike many HR executives with whom I'd worked in the past, Tracy approached the work from an extraordinarily strong business perspective. She didn't focus her efforts solely on the people aspect of our business; she became deeply knowledgeable about our products, our processes, and our finances. This intersection of talents proved to be an unbeatable combination. Her goal was not simply to attract and retain talent, to keep our workforce engaged and productive, nor just to manage risk. Her goal was always to create a culture of high performance that drove business results and shareholder value, and she brought a unique ability to do that.

This chapter will dip into the science behind our results. Tracy was relentless about our need to understand the science behind the approach to culture building. She believed a proper understanding would help us be more deliberate with our actions. I admit that we resisted at first, but Tracy knew her craft. She never missed an opportunity to remind us of the science. She framed executive decisions in the context of the culture we desired, and she cheered us on when we got it right. So, here is what we learned.

I began this chapter by acknowledging that culture represents the attitudes, beliefs, customs, rituals, and values shared by a community of people which lead those people to behave in specific ways. Thus, it follows that changing a culture would require a change to the attitudes, beliefs, customs, rituals, and values shared by that community of people, which would ultimately cause them to behave in new or different ways. Changing culture works, but it takes a long time.

Consider race relations in the United States. The Emancipation Proclamation was issued on January 1, 1863. Now, 150 years later, we are still fighting many of those old destructive attitudes, beliefs, and values—and the behaviors they drive.

There is a different way to change culture that is grounded in behavioral science. This is the approach that Tracy taught us to embrace, and it is based on the groundbreaking work of Aubrey C. Daniels, PhD, in his book, "Bringing out the Best in People."[4] This approach completely flips the method to culture change on its head. It prescribes that culture change can be accomplished very quickly if one focuses on the *behaviors* required to drive the desired culture. Essentially, this approach prescribes that you change behavior, not minds! From a behavioral perspective, the definition of culture is:

Culture is the pattern of behaviors that are reinforced or punished by people and by systems, over time.

It sounds simple, and it is—once you fully understand each element of the definition. First, behavioral changes require that you carefully identify the behaviors required to drive the culture to which you aspire. Next, you align your business practices, people practices, reinforcement processes, and human capital systems to reinforce them. Finally, you are relentless in ensuring that you maintain focus on this formula. You must truly walk your talk.

---

[4] Bringing out the Best in People by Aubrey C. Daniels

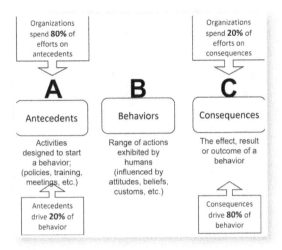

This principle is known as ABC, and it has been around since the days of B.F. Skinner and the beginning of the science of behavioral analysis. Antecedents (A) are those things we do to start a behavior (B). Consequences (C) are those things that result from that behavior.

When we began analyzing how things got done at HMS, we discovered that we spent plenty of time issuing policies, training, and communications about things we wanted from our workforce. These are all antecedents. But we also discovered that we spent little time thinking about how we would hold people accountable for those things. And we spent almost no time discussing the behaviors we were trying to drive with those edicts. This, we discovered, was not unusual—it's an oversight many organizations make.

So, we became disciplined. We began by defining the culture to which we aspired. Then, we engaged people throughout the organization to identify the key behaviors we needed from both employees and leaders to build that culture.

For this work, we relied heavily on the early practices of Dr. John Kotter. Dr. Kotter is internationally known and widely regarded as the foremost speaker on the topics of Leadership and Change. His is the premier voice for understanding how the best organizations achieve successful transformations. As the Konosuke Matsushita Professor of Leadership, Emeritus at the Harvard Business School, and a graduate of MIT and Harvard, Kotter's vast experience and knowledge on successful change and leadership have been proven time and again.

Dr. Kotter eventually became a significant partner in our transformation. But in the early days, we leaned on teachings from "Corporate Culture and Performance," the 1992 book he coauthored with James L. Heskett. [5]

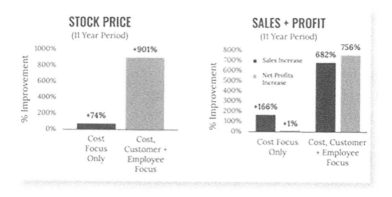

In this book, the authors shared the results from an 11-year study which showed the tremendous impact that culture has on performance. We wanted the same results.

In partnership with many of our employees, we defined the high-level behaviors that would characterize the culture we desired for our company.

By defining the behaviors ahead of time, we established clear guideposts to drive our actions and assess our progress on our journey.

---

[5]   Culture and Performance by Dr. John Kotter and James L. Heskett

Cultural Behaviors

Leader Behaviors	Employee Behaviors	Business Results
• Equal emphasis on employees, customers, and financials. • Direction is clear and all activity is linked to the organization's vision and strategy. • Employees are provided with the skills, tools, and authority to perform at high levels. • Positive reinforcement is more common than punishment.	• A clear line of sight from day-to-day work to customer value. • Knowledgeable about the business and its finances and able to make sound judgements. • Perform at high levels because they want to, not because they have to!	Sustained growth in: • Revenue • Operating Earnings • Stock Price • Earnings Per Share • Customer Satisfaction • Customer Retention • Employee Retention • Innovation

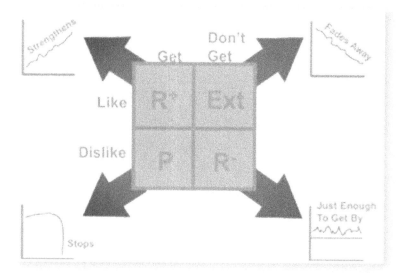

With clarity regarding the behaviors that would guide our culture, we turned our attention to consequences. That proved trickier because people have a visceral reaction to the word. Webster dictionary defines consequence as "a result or effect of an action or condition." But people tend to think of consequences as punishment. In fact, we learned there are four types of consequences: positive, negative, punishment, and extinction.

This exhibit illustrates those four types of consequences and the behavioral impact of each. Each has its place, but I won't get into detail about them here. Instead, I'll provide some great titles at the end of this book if you want to learn more.

At HMS, we didn't want a culture where people performed based on fear of punishment. We'd evolved away from that type of culture long ago. Rather, we aspired for a culture where people felt empowered to perform at high levels because it was the right thing to do. We focused our energies on positively reinforcing the behaviors that drove our culture and our success and connecting our workforce to the social value they created for those served by Medicaid.

This required a lot of discipline. We were trying to turn new skills into habits. The science says that positive reinforcement should occur ten times more frequently than negative reinforcement. Does your company do that? Or do you, like many of us, tend to react more strongly when something goes wrong? We were used to delivering edicts and being surprised when they didn't work. We focused more attention on poor performers than on great ones. Fortunately, Tracy reminded us to change our focus and to reinforce ourselves when we got it right (these principles work on executives too).

We spent a lot of time discussing reinforcement. In corporate America, people generally associate financial rewards with reinforcement. That is certainly one type of reinforcer, but it is not the only one. And in many cases, it is not the right one. The last thing you want is to create "coin-operated employees."

Reinforcement can take many forms. One of the most effective methods I've used is a personal outreach from me to an employee, acknowledging and thanking them for an action. Years later, I still hear people talk about the time they picked up the phone and it was me, or they opened an email from me, or I chatted with them in the elevator and asked what they did for the company (by the time I left HMS we had about 3,200 employees, so knowing everyone by name has become significantly more difficult). The impact of such simple gestures amazed me and taught me to never underestimate the value of a simple "Thank You." I also learned that our top performers needed regular and sincere reinforcement just as much as those who were only starting to get small wins.

Here is one example of the effectiveness of reinforcing the behaviors you want to drive. Compliance is critical in all businesses today, and that is especially true in the health care industry. It is also one of our core values. We were zealous about making our workforce understand—and live—that.

Our Chief Compliance and Ethics Officer and I decided to create Compliance Champions. This group consisted of employees across the company who would act as local contacts to help people with compliance related issues and to champion the cause of compliance and ethics. In the spirit of reinforcing positive behaviors (versus punishing bad behaviors), we decided to celebrate people who brought issues to our attention. So, whether an employee made a mistake, saw something incorrect, or just had a concern and reported it to Compliance, we celebrated them twice a year. Consistent with the science, our Compliance Champions group helped drive the behavior we wanted in the company. Employees became much more comfortable at identifying and reporting issues. Just think about an employee asking a co-worker about the plaque hanging in their cubicle. "How did you get that?" they'd ask. The answer: "I made a mistake and brought it to my manager's attention." Or: "I was celebrated for bringing something to the attention of Compliance." Think of the economic, ecological, and social impact if all employees across all industries were comfortable doing that!

At the risk of oversimplifying the science behind this approach, I will only introduce one more concept that had a profound impact on the development of our culture. Research shows there are three things that high-performing companies do fundamentally differently:

1. They actively and consciously build cultures that value employees, customers, and costs—and know how to make these values truly "live" for employees at all levels.
2. They execute their strategies with excellence.
3. They know how to create environments where people work at high levels because they *want to*, not because they *have to*.

These were the initial principles that drove everything we did.

The Customer
at the Center

O nce we'd gained clarity into the purposeful culture to which we aspired, and after we'd began to learn the craft behind it, we were ready to really begin the work.

That dedicated work started in 2012 when the executive team gathered to formally articulate the mission and values for the company. Remember, up until that point the entrepreneurial approach we had taken to growing our company meant that we shared a mission and a set of values that were not formally articulated but were simply understood by everyone. We needed to make these values explicit and then bring them to life for our workforce.

The process itself likely mirrored what corporations across the country do when they are defining or redefining their mission and values. We brought the executive team together, facilitated discussion, and spent a full day hashing it out.

What may have been different was that this time, we brought to the process a clarity about the kind of culture we wanted to drive. We also defined the high-level behaviors that would characterize this culture. From that starting point, we defined our mission and values.

Mission

To make healthcare better for everyone.

Through our industry-leading technology, analytics, and engagement solutions, we save billions of healthcare dollars annually while helping people lead healthier lives. Our broad range of payment accuracy and population health management solutions advance healthcare by helping healthcare organizations reduce costs and improve health outcomes.

Values

Customer Focus: We put the customer at the center of everything we do. We work relentlessly to build long-term relationships that deliver value to our customers and those they serve.

Results-driven collaboration: We reach across boundaries for diverse perspectives to create solutions that drive success.

Uncompromising Integrity: We operate in an open, fair, and honest manner, always striving to do what is right and earning the trust others place in us.

Absolute Accountability: We demand excellence in all we do, setting the highest standards and holding ourselves and each other accountable for achieving them.

Meaningful Innovation: We reach for original thinking and uncommon solutions that provide value to our customers and set us apart from our competitors.

Widespread Inclusion: We value inclusion of ideas, experiences, and backgrounds, and we actively seek to build a workforce that mirrors the communities we serve.

This session was also different because of our follow-up processes. In other companies where I had worked, we would leave such a meeting and go back to work. Afterwards, the communications folks would do a big roll-out of the new mission and values, complete with splashy posters and heartfelt videos. We did all of that, but we also kept it front and center in all interactions with employees. We specifically defined supporting behaviors for each of our values so that employees knew what it looked like to exhibit those values. We incorporated them into our performance review process, giving equal weight to results and behaviors when evaluating performance. We discussed and considered our values in business decisions we were making, and we took decisive action when an employee did not display them. Let me give you an example:

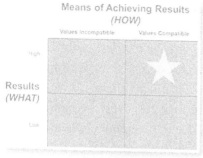

Means of Achieving Results (HOW)

Values Incompatible   Values Compatible

High

Results (WHAT)

Low

Our desired culture demanded that we be both value *and* values driven. In other words, while we certainly wanted to create value for our customers and our shareholders, we were also committed to creating that value in an ethical and moral manner that was unwaveringly consistent with the values we had established for ourselves. As a result, we had to focus not only on what people did, but also on how they did it. Based on this chart (which illustrates both the results an employee achieves and the degree to which he or she demonstrates the organization's values in the achievement of those results), we were able to look for what we referred to as "upper right" performance. Let me give you an example:

We had a senior level manager who consistently delivered top-tier results. He had great relationships with his customers. But his subordinates feared and disliked him. He was intimidating and rude, he created an atmosphere of fear in his department, and he seldom acknowledged the contributions of others. Turnover and employee relations issues in his department were high, and employee engagement and manager effectiveness were low. He managed metrics rather than driving behaviors. He created an "us against them" attitude toward other departments. In essence, his performance would have charted in the upper left corner of the above chart. We had tolerated his behavior for years because he delivered so consistently. But as one of our OD leaders frequently told us, "Employees don't look for proof that you mean what you say, they look for evidence that you don't." If we continued to tolerate this manager's behavior, we would be providing his colleagues with the evidence that our words did not matter.

Oh, we tried counseling first, but it had little impact. So, we fired him. And it sent shockwaves through the company. It was one of the most impactful decisions we made to underscore how serious we were. It was a painful decision which generated serious debate at the executive table. We paid a price for it, too, as we scrambled to mollify his clients and cover his results. But it was the right decision. Because if we weren't willing to walk our talk as the leaders of this company, I knew that we would be back to business as usual, meaning all our hard work would've just been another corporate exercise. Ask yourself: Do you have an employee whose behavior you tolerate because of the results they deliver? Does employing them match up with your organizational culture?

Next, we turned to strategy execution. Remember, high-performing organizations execute with excellence.

For our execution, we used a tool that was developed by Ned Morse and the late Jim Hilgren from Continuous Learning Group. [6]

This tool is called DCOM. It essentially identifies four core elements of execution:

- **Direction**: Are performers clear about the mission and strategy of the organization? Do they understand how their day-to-day work contributes to the organization's success?
- **Competence**: Do performers have the skills and knowledge required to succeed? Do they have the technical skills? Financial acumen? Strategic literacy?
- **Opportunity**: Do performers have the tools required to perform at high levels? Do they have appropriate time and technology? Appropriate levels of authority? Money and Materials? Information?
- **Motivation**: Do people perform at high levels because they want to or because they have to? Is positive reinforcement more common than punishment?

As this chart illustrates, you can achieve high performance results if you have all the elements in place. For each element missing, you will see specific, troubling symptoms in your organization.

---

[6] Ned Morse, CEO Continuous Learning Group; Author "SwitchPoints: Culture Change on the Fast Track to Business Success"

As this chart illustrates, if you have all the elements in place, you can achieve high performance results. For each element missing, you will see specific, troubling symptoms in your organization.

Direction	Competence	Opportunity	Motivation	Result
✗	✓	✓	✓	Chaos
✓	✗	✓	✓	Failure
✓	✓	✗	✓	Frustration
✓	✓	✓	✗	Lethargy
✓	✓	✓	✓	High Performance

DCOM was helpful to us—not just to guide our activities, but as a tool used to diagnose gaps both at the enterprise level and within specific business units. The results of gaps in any of these core elements are readily visible in organizations. A skilled OD consultant or leader can spend a few days observing a group of performers and get a good sense of where to probe more deeply to diagnose performance gaps and create corrective action plans.

We took much action to address gaps at the enterprise level. Early on, we focused a great deal on building strategic and financial literacy within the workforce. That work continues to this day, and I am immensely proud of how well our workforce understood our strategy and how effectively they considered the financial implications of both their individual actions and our organizational actions.

There are so many critical aspects of our cultural journey, I find it hard to pick one as most important. But this I can say with confidence: Leadership matters—and the executive leadership team plays an essential role in bringing culture to life.

Next, I will turn our attention to how we at HMS developed our executive team.

The Team Who Got You Here May Not Be Able to Get You There

I 've worked with several executive teams—first as I moved up the ladder into the executive ranks, and finally as President and CEO. These were mostly people I respected and whose contribution to company results I have greatly valued. But I have also come to believe that for every executive, there is a season—a time when the skills and attributes that person brings are exactly right for what the company needs. And it's only natural that there comes a time when that season ends—and that reality must be acknowledged and acted upon.

At HMS, this played out soon after we had established our mission and values. We had a new Human Resources leader, we were acknowledging the things we needed to improve to stay viable, and we were creating a purposeful culture—but not everyone on the executive team was on board.

There were several reasons for this. I discussed earlier how HMS began as a small entrepreneurial company. Often, the types of leaders who thrive in that kind of environment aren't as cooperative in a more structured and disciplined situation. We had reached a stage where we needed to add more consistency and discipline to our products and processes. We couldn't customize individual solutions for every customer; we had to determine how to create durable and configurable innovations to meet their needs. We could no longer rely on end-of-quarter heroics to meet our numbers, either. We were growing, and we had to change. Some of our executives weren't interested in the next part of our journey.

Others had simply peaked in their capabilities. They were good people who had served us well, but they simply were not equipped to take us to the next level. We all tried, but it became clear they were immersed in the ways of the past and could not perform in light of our new expectations. In some cases, they realized this on their own; in others, they had to be coached out. Some executives stayed and continued to be an integral part of our growth while no longer reporting directly to me. This speaks to the impact our company has on the healthcare system and the pride and love these executives still had for the company, the mission, and their co-workers.

Finally, there were those who simply didn't have the temperament required to take this cultural journey. They rolled their eyes at the notion of culture and wouldn't (or couldn't) bring it to life for our employees. They scoffed at what they considered "soft" conversations. They continued to reinforce the old way of doing things. This type of executive is by far the most difficult to deal with. They may nod and agree during executive meeting, then fail to execute on agreements. They may create factions within the executive team. They may even deliberately undermine the company's efforts within their individual organizations.

Saying goodbye to valued colleagues is never easy. It broke my heart to see some members of the team leave the company. But not when it was an executive who wouldn't get on board. I passionately believe that weeding out this type of executive was one of my most important roles. These leaders can create massive damage. They demoralize the whole organization and corrode the culture. That is intolerable. And there were times that I took too long to cut the cord, and employees saw that.

When an executive leaves an organization, he or she must be replaced. This provides a tremendous opportunity to create a high-performing culture—if one can avoid the pitfalls.

Tempting though it may be, you cannot fall into the age-old tendency of hiring in your own image. You also want to avoid hiring someone just because they have the right credentials or technical expertise.

An effective executive team is like a fine-tuned orchestra. Each member should complement the whole. When the opportunity to hire arises, you want to start by looking at the rest of the team. What strengths and character does each person brings? What gaps exist in experience and style? Is your team appropriately diverse? With these questions answered, you can begin to source candidates who will really strengthen the team. During the interview processes, in addition to the critical qualifications for the job, you also want to pay careful attention to your cultural requirements. What does this individual believe about the role of the workforce in the organization's success? What values do they express? How do they describe the cultures of the previous places they worked? What is their impression of the culture of your organization? Will they be comfortable within that culture and committed to bringing it to life?

We took this careful approach to hiring executives, and I'm pleased to say we won far more often than we lost. I am exceptionally proud of the executive team we built. And when I say *we*, I mean it. I didn't do it alone or just with our head of Human Resources. Every member of the executive team contributed to the sourcing process, the interviewing process, and the enculturation of our new executives.

And it didn't end once our new executives were on board. Every quarter, the executive team met offsite for a two-day strategy session, and part of every session was devoted to what we called "Executive Health." We worked with a consultant who has been a long-term confidant, friend and coach to me for many years. Debjani Biswas is the CEO and Founder of Coachieve LLC. She has particular expertise in innovation, inclusive leadership, and emotional intelligence, and she has authored two books: "Unleash the Power of Diversity" and "Miserably Successful No More." Debjani has been an inspiration in my life and a great coach, mentor, and overall advisor to me and my senior executive team. She has helped me navigate through various transitions in my leadership team and has provided us with the necessary tools to move from a "watch your back" to "have your back" culture. As CEO, it can be difficult to find someone to talk with who truly understands the connection between personal, emotional, and business acumen. Debjani does. Even though we were her client, I always knew she had my back. I consider her a true friend. She brought an expertise that we had long valued, but her role and contribution also evolved throughout our cultural journey. She remains an influence in my life and career today.

During these executive health sessions, we dug deep to examine how effectively we were working together. Our aim was to address issues and grievances within the team, assess how we were showing up to the organization, and to get to know one another on a deeper and more personal level. I often started these sessions by being vulnerable—

saying something about myself or how I should have acted in a situation, which allowed others to be vulnerable as well.

People confuse vulnerability with weakness. But if you consider being authentic with people you trust—people who have your back—as a weakness, then you'll never fully realize the strength and freedom it gives you, or the impact it has on the people you work with.

Remember that we were committed to taking a behavioral approach to culture development. What is expected of the workforce should also be expected of the executives in the organization. Early on, we worked together to create a list of executive behaviors that would articulate our commitment to "have each other's back."

Articulating behaviors is important—not just for the clarity it provides, but because it gives one a language for having difficult conversations. Let's face it. It's tough to stay the course all the time, especially with a team that is passionate about its work, its mission, its results, and its turf. There are natural conflicts between people and between departments, and it can be easy to lose your way in the heat of a moment. By anticipating and specifying the behaviors most critical to the team's unity, we were able to have calm and rational discussions when things went south.

HMS EXECUTIVE TEAM BEHAVIOR COMMITMENTS

- I think HMS first: functional, team, and personal positions take second place.
- I assume positive intent and ask "what else might be true" in the face of gut reactions.
- I bring problems to the table swiftly so we may solve issues in a non-judgmental manner. When things go wrong, I make it safe for all levels to share bad news without fear.
- I am a loyal advocate in your absence and do not tolerate behaviors that derail our team's unity.
- I am transparent and authentic and listen generously.
- I have the courage to disagree with you constructively and "listen as if I might be wrong."
- I honestly share my views for or against an issue with HMS' best interests in mind. No matter my original position, I will stand behind the team's decision 100% and support it with my actions and my words.

Like everything else about our cultural journey, instituting these commitments didn't come naturally. We had them laminated on cards which we kept on our desks. We had to remind ourselves of our commitments to one another and remember to reinforce them. Over time, these behaviors became habit. We became a more unified and cohesive executive team, but we also became more predictable to the workforce.

Of course, it's easy to forget some of these commitments when you're in a very engaged or heated conversation. But usually, if I find myself cutting someone off, I will apologize and say I should have listened generously. As the CEO, adopting these behaviors allowed others to show vulnerabilities and ask for reminders from the team when their own behavior strayed. As a leader, do you model the behaviors you espouse for your organization? Are you willing to be vulnerable?

This was not the only tool we used to deepen our effectiveness. Another tool we embraced was the DiSC personality profile, originally proposed by William Moulton Marston, a physiological psychologist with a Ph.D. from Harvard, and later refined by several psychologists to bring us its current format.

DiSC measures your personality and behavioral style. It describes human behavior in various situations, including how one responds to challenges, influences others, their preferred pace, and how one responds to rules and procedures. We found it useful for understanding individual executive styles and learning skills that allowed us to better interact with one another. As you may have guessed, our executive team included a lot of D's, which is not unusual. Dominance is something that has long been taught as a factor critical to success in American businesses. It's how you get ahead. We were taught to direct the outcomes we want.

As we learned the value of different styles, we began to cherish those who brought other styles for the balance they created. The DiSC tool also served as a reference point when bringing on new executives. The last thing you want is a team full of D's—that runs the risk of everyone talking and no one listening. You need Influencers to promote and sell your ideas, the Steadiness of the S personalities to build structure and accommodate change, and the Conscientiousness of the C personalities to hold you accountable with analytics and processes.

Because of the value it brought to executives, we cascaded this tool throughout the organization. It became valuable for work teams, project groups, and for when we brought people together to perform. Today, we have an internal team of talented facilitators who can administer and debrief this tool for any employee who is interested in learning more about themselves.

The final tool we deeply embraced was EQ-i, a model for emotional intelligence. Emotional intelligence skills are critical for leadership, team effectiveness, work performance, influence, work/life balance, and wellbeing.

The fifteen competencies in the scientifically validated EQ-i 2.0 model are highly correlated with inspirational leadership, innovative work cultures, highly effective teams, and engaged and committed talent. These are all learned skills that we can develop and improve!

I first completed EQ-i in 2016. At that time, my highest scores were in self-actualization, optimism, and problem solving.

Self-actualization is one's willingness to persistently try to improve themselves and engage in the pursuit of personally relevant and meaningful objectives that lead to a rich and enjoyable life.

Optimism is an indicator of one's positive attitude and outlook on life. It involves remaining hopeful and resilient—despite occasional setbacks.

Problem solving is the ability to find solutions to problems in situations where emotions are involved. Problem solving includes the ability to understand how emotions impact decision making.

My lowest scores were in impulse control, interpersonal relationships, and self-regard. Impulse control is the ability to resist or delay an impulse, drive, or temptation to act. It involves avoiding rash behaviors and decision making.

Interpersonal relationships refers to the skill of developing and maintaining mutually satisfying relationships that are characterized by trust and compassion.

Self-regard is respecting oneself while understanding and accepting one's strengths and weaknesses. Self-regard is often associated with feelings of inner strength and self-confidence.

For the most part, these scores made sense to me. My strengths were consistent with the skills that made me a student of the business and prompted my rapid career progression. Because I was an innate dot-connector, I was highly skilled at solving problems. My weaknesses could be rationalized when I considered the challenges of my upbringing and my personal self-esteem issues. Best of all, knowledge of this gave me a focus for my development efforts. Discussing my results openly with my executive team (as they did with their own) gave me a cadre of support. It's very powerful to give people the opening to help you improve yourself.

Interestingly, I completed the EQ-i for a second time in 2019 with some marked differences in scores. In terms of strengths, self-actualization remained in the top three, but social responsibility and flexibility had moved into the other two top spots. I don't think it was because I'd become less optimistic or a less effective problem solver. I believe it was because I worried less about the day-to-day work of the company as my executive team became more cohesive and our organization more engaged. I had more time to turn outward and focus on the differences we were making in the lives of our customers and the communities we served, and more time to engage with shareholders and other stakeholders.

In terms of my lowest scores, impulse control and self-regard remained (life-long battles for those two, I fear), but stress tolerance dropped. Stress tolerance involves coping with stressful or difficult situations and believing that one can manage or influence situations in a positive manner. This is a skill upon which I had always prided myself. However, I believe that this helps to illustrate the situational nature of emotional intelligence. I completed this instrument for the second time during a particularly stressful period. I was having some health issues and facing surgery. I was also in the process of saying goodbye to a leader I had nurtured and supported for years. My stress was reflected in my scores.

Knowing this—and sharing it with others—helped me get through those days. I cannot overstate the value of exploring oneself to build leadership effectiveness—and the significance of knowing one's peers deeply. I could recount dozens of conversations with my direct reports where we referenced our individual strengths and weaknesses to problem solve, construct balanced executive sponsorship assignments, resolve conflicts, and support one another through challenging times.

Now that I'm semi-retired and have left HMS, I think my scores would be even more different. After all, I'm focused on the next chapter of my life with excitement, uncertainty, and hope.

These were the tools we selected. They were effective, but there was nothing magical about them. There are many equally effective tools out there. The real question to consider is what you are doing to build the effectiveness of your executive team. If you're doing nothing, please reconsider. I believe this work is just as important for creating a high-performance culture as reviewing your business results.

We built one of the strongest executive teams in the business—a team who shared my commitment to lead from the head *and* the heart. Our team can proudly take equal credit for the highly engaged, high-performing workforce we empowered—and ultimately, for the results we generated together.

Our Big Opportunity

In 2015, we were proud of the progress we were making but a bit impatient about the pace. We had implemented several new processes that increased the discipline and effectiveness of our business. We were building a strong and effective executive team. We had created new management information systems that gave us data to better manage our business. We had put new financial controls in place. We'd constructed configurable product structures that allowed us to meet customer needs while still efficiently managing product administration. We'd adopted a balanced scorecard to ensure that we were paying appropriate attention to customers, costs, and employees. We'd implemented our first employee engagement survey in 2013, which provided us with a baseline of our effectiveness for managing our workforce. We had seen minor increases in engagement in the two years since we started our journey. Yet we remained convinced that we could move faster. The question was: how?

At this same time, we were about to implement a new strategy. Our basic blocking and tackling were in place, so it was time to create a framework for growth. We based our strategy on "The Alchemy of Growth: Practical Insights for Building the Enduring Enterprise" by Mehrdad Baghai, Steve Coley and David White.[7]

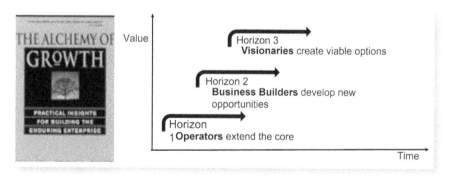

Our strategy (based around their guidelines) would enable us to prioritize investments to strengthen our core business, expand by advancing new products and services, and ultimately generate a

7   "The Alchemy of Growth: Practical Insights for Building the Enduring Enterprise" by Mehrdad Baghai, Steve Coley and David White.

pipeline of industry-leading innovations. We believed that our strategy was solid, and we were investing in the technology, acquisitions, and talent to advance it.

For decades, we had relied on our core product line to drive growth. And while it was still going strong, all businesses ultimately decline as growth slows. We knew it was time to prepare for the future, and the Three Horizon's model from "The Alchemy of Growth" fit our needs perfectly. Horizon One would ensure that we kept our critical core business healthy and prosperous while expanding margins. Horizon Two would drive us to focus on building new businesses that could eventually supplement or even replace our core business. Horizon Three encouraged us to imagine a new future. Operating as a type of "think tank" concept, this horizon allowed us to rapidly experiment and innovate—we would fail fast and identify the products and services of tomorrow, whether through development or acquisition.

We were excited about and committed to this strategy. The model resonated with both our executive team and the workforce. It was easy to explain, and it created a language for strategy in the business.

We still had a couple of problems to solve. Because of our commitment to strategic and financial literacy, we wanted our entire workforce to deeply understand our strategy and the value behind it. We also wanted to intensely engage our workforce in its execution. Oh, and we wanted to move fast.

When faced with these challenges, many companies would create teams focused on each horizon (think NewCo.—a common strategy for assembling and segregating a team to focus on next generation products and services often deployed by established companies). We didn't want to do that because we didn't want to create factions where people were focused on only one horizon. We believed doing that would inevitably result in unhealthy competition and turf wars—and perhaps even a feeling that one horizon was "cooler" than another.

Clearly, we needed a new model for change that could solve these problems and allow us to move fast.

 Our research led us to an old friend. It turns out Dr. John Kotter had released a new book in 2014 called "Accelerate: Building Strategic Agility for a Faster-Moving World." In Dr. Kotter's own words, "Accelerate is about how to handle strategic challenges fast enough, with agility and creativity, to take advantage of windows of opportunity that open and shut more quickly today. It shows how people in some leading innovative organizations move ahead of fierce competition, deal with unprecedented turmoil, and cope with the threat of technological discontinuities—all without sacrificing short term results or wearing out their workforces."[8]

We were intrigued. We bought the book (as we had done with many of Dr. Kotter's books over the years) and picked up some great ideas. But we wanted more. Our Organizational Development lead (and my co-author, Deborah Kelly) signed up for a free seminar being delivered by the company Dr. Kotter had founded in 2008 (Kotter International—now simply called Kotter). Unfortunately, the seminar was full, and she couldn't get in. However, she discovered it was being delivered by a colleague Deb had worked with for many years. In our "it's not *what* you know, it's *who* you know" world, she immediately reached out to him to see if we could gain additional insights.

Mind you, we were not looking to enter an engagement with Kotter International at this time. We were not a company that routinely brought in consultants to solve our problems. I may be a bit jaded, but I often felt that consultants just told me what I already knew (or in other words, they borrowed my watch to tell me what time it was!) We hoped that with a little more guidance, we could execute this change model on our own.

---

[8] "Accelerate: Building Strategic Agility for a Faster-Moving World" by Dr. John Kotter

Deb contacted David Carder. As a Managing Director for Kotter, David serves as the lead consultant on many of Kotter's largest client engagements. He's also worked across a range of industries including energy, healthcare, financial services, defense, aerospace, and nonprofit. Throughout his entire career, David has focused on unleashing the potential of leaders to drive organizational transformations. He graciously agreed to spend some time with Deb to provide more details about the Kotter approach. They agreed it would also be valuable to educate the executive leadership team about Kotter's principles and the process that drove those principles. So, we invited David to spend several hours with us at our next Executive Strategy meeting. That session proved to be a turning point in our cultural evolution.

As David spoke about the principles behind Kotter's transformation model, I swear you could see lightbulbs flashing all around the room. David is a skilled facilitator with an uncanny ability to grasp the complexities of the business and uncover the unspoken motivations and concerns certain groups. But it was much more than that—his passion for his work, and his approach, clearly came from a profound belief in the work he was doing and the value it provided. That spoke directly to myself and many others in the room. By the end of this meeting, we'd decided we wanted to move forward with this approach, and we were to do so directly with Kotter International. While working long term with external consultants was not part of our company DNA, we all realized there was something special there—and that we would be stronger together than alone.

Interestingly, this was not a typical consulting engagement where we decided to move forward and then signed a contract. Dr. Kotter is in a phase of his career where his interest goes well beyond the financial. He wanted to work with companies that were doing meaningful work, would further his body of exploration, provide a laboratory for implementing his research, and bring the commitment and the heart to see it to completion. Naturally, this made us even more eager to work with him and his team. After the meeting with David, several members of the executive team and I spent time with Dr. Kotter and his team. We ultimately decided our two companies would be a good match.

This was not an unsubstantial investment. Tracy South and Deb Kelly were so convinced that it was the right course of action that they sat with our Chief Financial Officer and promised him a 10x return on our investment. I'm pleased to say that they more than delivered on that—and the financial ROI was but a small part of the value we gained. In April of 2015, we signed a contract and began our journey with Kotter.

We were also introduced to another consummate professional who would join our team. Jimmy Leppert was a Managing Director at Kotter with an impressive resume. He helps leaders bring speed and scale to the implementation of their most pressing strategic priorities. Jimmy has worked with two of the most well recognized business gurus in the world, completing an "old school" apprenticeship with Peter Senge at MIT and now working with John Kotter. He has studied leading systemic change at Harvard and teaching/learning at the University of Virginia. Through these experiences, Jimmy has worked with leaders in virtually every industry in every corner of the world. Jimmy was Kotter's "feet on the ground" at HMS, and he became a trusted and valued partner and friend.

Before I explain our journey with the Kotter organization in detail, I'd like to mention that we didn't consider this to be a change in our approach to our culture strategy. Rather, we saw this as a continuation of the work we had begun in 2012. We didn't simply follow the Kotter roadmap, we integrated it into our approach and made it our own. We didn't turn over ownership or accountability for results to our Kotter colleagues. We were active partners with perspectives, opinions, and beliefs of our own. We were committed to taking a holistic approach, and we interwove every policy and business practice to drive the high-performance culture we desired. I think that is why we saw such astonishing results, and I don't think I'm being overly presumptuous when I say that I'm convinced Kotter learned from us as we learned from them.

We also knew from the beginning that we wanted to measure outcomes. Not only would that be critical to gaining leadership and board acceptance, but we believed in our work and wanted to show that it was making a difference. We put a number of metrics in place to measure both human capital and business implications, and we persistently measured our progress against those. We partnered with our finance team (who are often among the most vocal skeptics about such efforts) and asked them to validate and value both hard and soft results.

As our efforts revealed tangible results month after month, it was interesting to watch skeptical leaders (and finance partners) begin to embrace this approach. Our Board of Directors went from viewing this as a workplace morale initiative to actively supporting it as a business initiative that yielded tangible business results. Eventually, they were talking it up with other companies at which they served.

It's important that you understand this before we dive into our journey with Kotter. Too many companies look to external consultants to come in and solve their problems *for* them instead of *with* them. But I contend that you must own it and commit to it. You must put measures in place to prove that it works, and you must align the engagement around your entire business and human capital strategy to get the best results. That's what we did—and that's why it worked.

KOTTER'S 8-STEP PROCESS

Kotter's process consists of 8-steps, all centered around a big opportunity. This was meaningful to me, because I come from an era where change initiatives were often driven by a concept known as "a burning platform." The burning platform is a term used to describe the process of helping people see the dire consequences of not changing. By sparking just enough concern for what happens if the status quo remains the same, people embrace change. At least, that's the theory. But Dr. Kotter had a different view.

While fear can be a motivator, Kotter believes that it fails to motivate the actions and behaviors that drive sustained change. According to a Forbes article "Why Burning Platforms Don't Work" by Kotter contributor Gaurav Gupta:

> *Research has shown that fear leads people to be more conservative—taking fewer risks and preserving the status quo. Activating fear in people makes them less likely to want to change the current situation. Gregory Berns, director at the Center of Neuropolicy at Emory University, says 'The most concrete thing that neuroscience tells us is that when the fear system of the brain is active, exploratory activity and risk-taking are turned off.' As a result, a lot of energy gets directed at justifying the status quo and pushing back against the need for real change.*[9]

Far better, Kotter says, is to:

> *frame the need to change in the context of a positive 'big opportunity'. Opportunity-driven urgency engenders dynamic, positive, and directional energy and pro-activity. It enables*

---

[9] "Why Burning Platforms Don't Work" by Gaurav Gupta

Leading with Your Head and Your Heart

sustainable action. This is about winning hearts as well as minds. A big opportunity should be emotionally compelling and motivating, but link to a change vision that gives a clear picture of what is needed to realize the opportunity, and a strategy that creates the path to success.

I shared this view. In my early days at HMS, I was charged with improving the financial results of subsidiaries and trying to spark growth and advance the cultural agenda at the company. We did have a burning platform—we were threatened to be de-listed off NASDAQ, our stock had dropped to 57 cents a share, and there was no definable and defensible strategy. In my corner of the world, I believed that I could instill hope, vision, and a way to grow the businesses I'd been tasked with running.

I focused my teams on the opportunity we had rather than the threat we faced, and it was a big reason why HMS weathered that storm and ultimately became the company we're so proud of today. I remember coaching people through those difficult times and seeing hope in their faces. They knew we could build something special. Engaging them to dream of the potential of what can be was much more inspiring—and fulfilling—than telling them what to do and how to do it.

So, Kotter's view made perfect sense to us. We were already committed to avoiding a fear-based culture. We were determined to create an environment where people performed at high levels because they *wanted* to, not because they *had* to. And we had an emerging strategy that laid out a path to success. Thus, our first step with Kotter was to create HMS's Big Opportunity.

> **The Big Opportunity**
> The healthcare system is under siege. With ever-rising costs, everyone is at risk.
>
> WE ARE HMS!
>
> We have the data, technology, and know-how to unlock vital healthcare resources--and the track record to prove it to our customers and those they serve.
>
> We are the Good Guys and we want the world to know...*because everything we do matters!*
>
> **GOOD GUYS**

This proved to be an exhilarating experience. Looking back on it, I recall it as the first time this executive team really came together in passion and commitment for the future of our company. The excitement in the room was palpable. Everyone shared their visions of what was possible and how each of their businesses would contribute. Two of the executives were brand new—in fact, one was in his first week. Yet *everyone* contributed. Everyone felt heard, and we easily crafted a statement that we all felt perfectly articulated the opportunity we had ahead of us. Each word meant something to all of us, yet we avoided the nitpicking and wordsmithing that often accompanies such efforts. We concluded that meeting radiating pure optimism.

In the past, this type of meeting would have taken three days. People would have worried about grammar and form versus substance. But this time, it was incredibly easy to lock arms and agree that our Big Opportunity was extremely powerful.

CREATING URGENCY

Our next step in the journey was to communicate our opportunity and create a sense of urgency within our workforce. Dr. Kotter has a very specific definition of urgency, which he takes care to painstakingly explain. In fact, he wrote an entire book about it, called "A Sense of Urgency." [10] It's well worth the read.

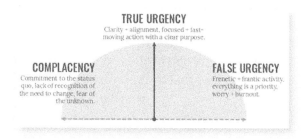

Complacency is often seen in companies who are satisfied with the status quo. When companies are complacent, we hear phrases like "we've always done it this way" or "why make a change when the old way still works?" Urgency is the opposite of complacency. Urgency

---

[10] "A Sense of Urgency" by Dr. John Kotter

Leading with Your Head and Your Heart

helps employees see the need for change. Complacency is the enemy of urgency, Dr. Kotter asserts.

Many companies insist they operate with a sense of urgency. They point to their crowded calendars, the never-ending meetings, and their overwhelmed and overworked employees as proof. This, Dr. Kotter explains, is what is known as false urgency. False urgency is rooted in anxiety and creates a lot of activity without productive results. It is often created by pressure from above, with actions that are not aimed at the true goal. Employees get burned out from constant false urgency. I've worked with leaders who use false urgency as a motivator, not realizing that what they are truly doing is *demotivating*.

Real urgency, according to Dr. Kotter, is a combination of thoughts, feelings, and actual behavior. It's when employees believe there are great opportunities out there as well as great hazards. Employees feel a gut-level determination that we're going to do something immediately to win. Each employee has a hyper-alertness to what's going on. They come to work every day with a commitment to making something happen and moving their company closer to achieving its big opportunity. I can proudly say that we achieved that at HMS, and our employees stepped up to help lead the way.

THE URGENCY TEAM

As you might guess, Kotter has a method for achieving real urgency. So, our next step was to create our Urgency Team. This team was comprised of 40-50 hand-picked employees, emphasizing a diversity of functions, departments, levels, and geographic locations. What they had in common was that each was a high performer, a recognized leader among their peers, with a strong sense of enthusiasm and minimal ego. We wanted a team that would work for the overall good of the organization rather than for personal recognition or gain. The executive team reached out to them with personal phone calls and briefly explained what we wanted to do as we asked them to participate.

Honestly, none of them knew what they were getting themselves into, nor did they fully understand what we were asking. Heck, *we* not sure we knew what was coming. But because they were who they were, they all enthusiastically agreed. Within weeks of developing our Big Opportunity statement, we brought them together at our Corporate Headquarters for a two-day kick-off meeting.

The goal of this meeting wasn't simply to engage this group of people in our Big Opportunity and the strategy that would enable it. It was also to ask them to educate the entire workforce about it and then invite every employee in the company to become an active participant in achieving it. Because real urgency requires a critical mass of the organization, their goal was to get 50% plus 1 members of our workforce to raise their hands and agree to be part of this movement. How were they to do that? That was up to them. Kotter was there to facilitate the process; the executive team was there to establish the challenge, to clear obstacles, and to cheer them on. But the "how" was theirs to craft.

I began to see what urgency really looks like at that meeting. The Urgency Team was on fire. They instantly designed an approach and structure for achieving their goal. If fact, they decided that 50% plus 1 wasn't aggressive enough—instead, they established a stretch goal of 60% for themselves. They organized themselves into sub-teams and got to work. They reached out to the rest of the organization for expertise they didn't have on the team. They began recruiting other employees in hallways and the lunchroom during breaks. By the time the session ended at the end of the second day, they had created a website to manage the effort, they had posters in the elevators and hallways, they had a detailed plan to move forward, and they had already recruited over 100 employees to join what became known as the Volunteer Army. Most significantly, they had formed relationships with one another that have stood the test of time. They knew what they were accomplishing was different, and excitement was in the air!

This wasn't business as usual. It wasn't a slick corporate communications campaign. The Urgency Team didn't rely on our established support

Leading with Your Head and Your Heart

functions to get things done. They didn't want to wait in queue until these groups had time to work with them. It was a true grassroots effort. They reached out to the executive team and asked them to create selfie videos sharing their excitement about this journey, then they solicited volunteers with the skills to edit and distribute them. (That was when we all learned to hold our phones horizontally to film ourselves—to this day, I still sometimes forget!)

This led to series of videos from executives and a number of what I fondly called "CEO humiliation videos." I would dress in whatever costume fit the occasion and help employees create impactful videos that were fun and which got our message across. All our executives participated in producing these videos, operating outside of their comfort zones, and creating cultural memories that still resonate with the workforce. It also helped employees connect with me—and with other members of the executive team—as genuine people.

These efforts were not always well-received by the functions who had long provided such services to the organization. We had to stop the Facilities Team from taking down the posters in the elevators because they weren't adhered correctly. The Urgency Team had to field a "cease and desist" order from Marketing because their videos and marketing materials did not meet corporate standards. Kotter informed us this was not unusual. In the initial phases of his movement, most organizations run into factions within the company who are either comfortable with the status quo, threatened by impending change, or simply not interested in taking the journey. In fact, Dr. Kotter wrote a fable version of the "Accelerate" process called "That's Not How We Do It Here: How Organizations Rise and Fall—and Can Rise Again" with coauthor Holger Rathgeber.[11] This book portrays a clan of Meerkats facing big change to illustrate the principles of Accelerate and to

---

[11] "That's Not How We Do It Here: How Organizations Rise and Fall—and Can Rise Again" by John Kotter and Holger Rathgeber

discuss the soul-crushing feeling some employees experience when the response to their new ideas is, "That's not how we do it here."

The Urgency Team weathered these initial challenges with committed persistence and an unwavering support from the executive team. As they began to understand the reactions the workforce would experience, they decided to purchase a copy of "That's Not How We Do It Here" for every employee. Eventually, that clan of Meerkats became honorary members of the HMS workforce.

Once the kick-off meeting was over, the Urgency Team launched into full gear. They accelerated their efforts to educate the workforce on the HMS Big Opportunity and our strategy. They hosted an all-employee event to formally introduce the movement and build excitement across the country. They used creative and innovative approaches to recruit additional employees into the Volunteer Army. They requested (and received) a small budget to fund tokens to recognize participation. They attended team meetings and huddles, filmed, edited, and distributed inspirational videos, and wore buttons that said "TBO: Ask Me!" As for the executive team, we tapped into our cultural model to regularly and enthusiastically reinforce their actions to build urgency, and we taught our senior leaders to do the same. Within six weeks, this team had achieved their goal of enrolling 50% plus 1 of our employees in the Volunteer Army. Eight weeks after that, 60% of the workforce had raised their hands to say they wanted to actively participate in this journey.

Our first Urgency Team proved to be invaluable. But I'd be remiss if I made it seem as if it was all smooth sailing. In the beginning, there was a lot of cautious skepticism. The team knew it felt different, but they still needed to be convinced and reminded through leader behavior that this wasn't just another "program of the week" that would go away when the next "next thing" came along. Don't start such a journey unless you are committed to finishing it—or you risk breaking the hearts of your workforce.

TBO PRINCIPLES

This is probably the right place to point out that the Kotter process is centered around four key principles, which we adopted as our own and which have become an integrated part of our company's DNA. These principles resonated with me from the beginning because they were aligned with our values and my personal leadership style.

While Dr. Kotter references these principles throughout many of his books, he formally named the 4 Change Principles for the first time in his HBR article, "Accelerate," which preceded his book of the same name. He describes the four principles as follows:

Few vs. Many: You need more eyes to see, more brains to think, and more hands and feet to act. More people need to be able to make change happen—not just carry out someone else's directives. This must be done in a way that does not create chaos, create destructive conflict, duplicate efforts, or waste money. Done right, this uncovers leaders at all levels of the organization—ones you never knew you had.

For us, the Few vs. Many principle accomplished just that. We have seen leaders rise throughout the organization by being part of our TBO (The Big Opportunity) initiatives. In fact, this was more effective than any other leadership development program we had ever developed or delivered. I would add, again, the distinction between leadership and management. You could be a sole contributor and working in a call center or the mailroom and become a leader through this journey – you need not be a manager of people.

Have To vs. Want To: People who feel they have the opportunity to be involved in an important activity have shown that they will volunteer to do so in addition to their normal responsibilities. You don't have to hire new people; your existing people provide the energy—if you invite them. After all, it is your people who know where the pain points are and how to get things done.

From my perspective, this is where companies go wrong when they overtax the "few." Google allows employees to spend about 20% of their time on initiatives within their division and which they're passionate about. We have tried to capture the spirit of this in our culture by allowing employees to volunteer anywhere within the company. Thus, we felt that we were in good company with the likes of Google.

Head & Heart: Data and reason underpin many good ideas. But most people won't be inspired to help you if you appeal to logic alone. You must also appeal to how people feel—speak to the genuine and fundamental human desire to contribute to some bigger cause, to take an organization or community into a better future. Answer the questions burning in people's minds: "What's in it for me?" and "In service of what?" If you can provide a vehicle that gives greater meaning and purpose to an effort, extraordinary results are possible.

People want to belong to something with a bigger purpose. That's what has driven my career at HMS: my visits to public and children's hospitals in my first role at the company; the work we do to help the less fortunate by protecting our nation's Medicaid program; our helping to keep healthcare accessible and affordable for all commercial customers; and our assisting people to better manage outcomes through engagement. All of these practices help save lives! This motivates me and the HMS workforce!

Management & Leadership: To capitalize on windows of opportunity that might open and close quickly, the name of the game is leadership, and not just from one executive. It's about vision, opportunity, inspired action, innovation, and celebration—rather than just the essential managerial processes like project management, budget reviews and accountability to a plan. If you add the value of management to the value of leadership, you get 1 + 1 = 3.

Through the Results Accelerators, TBO initiatives, and our Guiding Coalition, HMS employees learn how to become leaders or improve their leadership skills. They are mentored by executives throughout this process, and we take special care to differentiate for them the differences between leadership and management. We also help them discern when each approach is warranted.

You can see the synergy of these principles in the vision and values we created at the beginning of our cultural journey. Some of them may even have come from our early studies of Dr. Kotter's work. The Hope painting outside of my office underscored my desire to do work that served others. But one of the new lines of thought to me was that of the Few vs. Many principle. Like many executives, I had come to rely on a small group of senior leaders I knew well and whose work I respected when something needed to get done. As our company grew, there were hundreds of people I didn't know. What kind of talent, I wondered, might be buried in our organization, untested, unchallenged, and uninspired? What might we discover if we could unlock that talent? I finally recognized that, as a leadership team, we were much more skilled at management than at leadership. So, we began to work on that as we developed our new executive team. What benefits could we reap if we built those same skills throughout the organization? For all these reasons, Dr. Kotter's 4 Change Principles, which we call TBO Principles, became as important as our corporate values.

THE VOLUNTEER ARMY

A majority of our employees were now eager to participate in the execution of our new strategy and the achievement of our Big Opportunity. However, that simply meant they had volunteered to help. We hadn't actually engaged them in any meaningful action beyond the creation of the Army. How to deploy them? The best way to understand next steps is to learn about what Dr. Kotter refers to as "the dual organization."

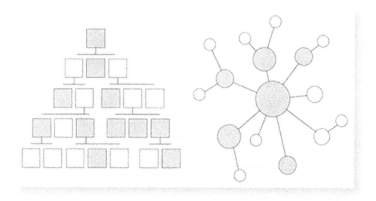

Virtually all successful organizations go through a remarkably similar lifecycle. They begin much the way HMS did in its early stage—with a group of entrepreneurs united around a vision. Each employee wears many hats. Structures are loose and communication is informal. Ideas can come from anyone. Dr. Kotter calls this a "network organization." As a company grows, there comes a time when that must change, as it did for HMS at the beginning of our cultural journey. The need for more formal processes and controls meant that we had to evolve into a more conventional hierarchical organization. For a while, companies going through this phase of their evolution are able to maintain both structures. But over time, the network organization inevitably shrinks, and the hierarchal organization takes over. That's unfortunate. Hierarchical management systems are designed for efficiency rather than strategic agility. While hierarchies are useful for managing the tactical challenges of running large enterprises, they are limited in their capacity to quickly spot hazards and opportunities, nimbly formulate strategic options, and rapidly execute responsive action.

Some organizations try to solve this problem by creating separate organizations: one focused on running the business while the other operates as a start-up, innovating and creating transformative businesses. I discussed earlier why I didn't think that would be a workable option for us.

Kotter's solution for a more dynamic approach to addressing the challenges of rapid change is the adoption of a dual operating system. This is accomplished by creating a second agile network structure that complements the traditional hierarchical organization. This second structure is not a cross-functional task force that reports to an executive champion. Rather, it's a relatively autonomous system that is free from the usual bureaucratic processes that slow organizations down. The participants in the network are drawn from and continue to work in the hierarchical structure. They serve as the catalysts for maintaining the necessary synergies between the two systems. Thus, the goal for our Volunteer Army would be to serve as this agile network structure.

At HMS, we adopted this concept but renamed the hierarchal organization the "Sustaining" organization and our network the "Transforming" organization. By joining the Volunteer Army, employees were invited to move in and out of the Transforming organization, where they could:

- Pursue broad enterprise missions about which they were passionate
- Collaborate with people they would not normally have in their regular jobs
- Increase their visibility and reach in the organization
- Bring innovation back into the sustaining organization
- Grow their leadership skills
- Make a real difference in the company

The Urgency Team expanded the TBO website (initially created by volunteers within the first week of kicking off this effort) to allow employees at all levels to seek volunteers for a variety of opportunities.

When a request was entered into the system, it was immediately dispatched to every member of the Volunteer Army. Managers requested volunteers to clear backlogs, the Urgency Team sought volunteers to source enterprise activities, other teams used it to find specialty skills required to complete a project, and employees used it to find mentors or support for learning new skills. From the very beginning, the response was inspiring. Within minutes of a request going out, we had dozens or even hundreds of volunteers seeking to fill said request. And no request was too mundane. I would sometimes see a volunteer request and wonder "Who would want to do that?" only to find that many people were eager and willing. Mind you, people were not doing this instead of their regular jobs—they were doing it in addition to the activities that filled their busy days. This was discretionary effort at its best. It was a true embodiment of our cultural goal of having people perform at high levels because they *wanted* to, not because they *had* to. Another benefit, from my perspective, is that the executive team and I had the honor of uncovering talent much deeper in the organization than we ever had before. We were continually astonished by the skill and passion we were discovering— and the high performance it drove!

One notable example of how impactful volunteer efforts were is illustrated in the example below.

A long-term mailroom employee wanted to impact AEBITDA. He took it upon himself to study each customer contract to identify which communications required overnight mail, regular delivery, and which could be replaced with email. During this process, he and his team of volunteers identified more than $1 million dollars in incremental, annualized savings. How's that for initiative? Would you be comfortable taking such action in your organization? Would your employees feel empowered to take it on?

GENERATE
Short-Term
Wins

WHY SHORT-TERM WINS ARE
IMPORTANT
- Prove it's worthwhile
- Reward efforts
- Fine tune strategy
- Undermine cynics
- Keep Executives engaged
- Reinvigorate the effort
- Build Momentum

Another important component of Kotter's 8-step process for accelerating change is to generate short-term wins. Why is this important? As a CEO who is driven by both head and heart, I began to see the value of our investment from the very beginning. I could see that we had unleashed the passions of our workforce. I could see commitment and morale improving. I could see the discretionary effort employees were putting forth. But other members on my executive team measure—and the same is true for most executive teams—valued primarily in terms of dollars and cents. For those executives, proof of concept requires fast financial results.

Kotter's solution to that is what he calls Results Accelerators. Results Accelerators focus on strategically important initiatives. They are quick sprints, comprised of small teams of employees who are hand-selected for their expertise and charged with delivering nearly impossible—but achievable—results in 90 days.

Getting people at the top to buy in required creating conditions for a highly engaged workforce to be activated around the right business metrics at the right time. Having highly quantifiable indicators of success meant executives who had not fully "bought-in" to our strategy only had to suspend disbelief for weeks—not months or years—to see if better results would be generated. Thus, Results Accelerators were a critical part of our "proof of concept."

Deceptively simple in execution, there is intricate design behind the concept. While the Kotter team brought that expertise in the beginning, they ultimately taught us to manage the process ourselves. (Incidentally, this was a significant difference between Kotter and many other consulting companies with whom I'd worked. Their commitment from the start helped transfer skills to our team, meaning we were not perpetually dependent on them.)

The Results Accelerator process starts by identifying strategically important challenges your company either has not been able to successfully solve or hasn't had the bandwidth to tackle. From that list, you select initiatives in which you believe you can gain traction in 90 days. Initially, our executive team made these selections. Subsequently, we expanded that group to include the rest of our senior leadership team to ensure more depth in our selections.

Once the selection of initiatives is complete, you choose an executive sponsor and a team leader. Together, they create a charter for each initiative to outline the problem they are charged with solving, along with the scope and boundaries of the challenge. Based on that data, they identify employees with the technical expertise, drive, and heart to get the job done.

While selecting the RA teams, we are careful to honor the "Few vs. Many" principle. Rather than simply selecting the same "obvious suspects" to fill roles, we reached down into the organization and solicited recommendations for people we didn't yet know. We looked for expertise, but we also sought a balance of style and temperament. We tried to find a mix of people who were led by the head as well as those who were led by the heart.

Once we had selected the team, we invited them to participate. Participation was on a "want to" basis. There was no pressure to participate, nor any penalty for choosing not to. It was an intense 90-day commitment, and we knew people would have fair reasons to opt out. What continued to amaze me, even as we were years into this approach, was how few people declined. In fact, people at all levels of the organization clamored to participate. We got requests, and we saw participation in a Results Accelerator as part of employees' development plans. Why? What was in it for them? There was no project bonus or monetary award at the end of these 90-day sprints.

I believe people wanted to participate because they truly wanted to solve vexing problems that had frustrated them. They wanted to build strong networks across the organization. They wanted unfettered access to the senior leadership team. But most of all, they cared.

Results Accelerator teams kick off with a two-day face-to-face session. The team arrives knowing little more than what is contained in the charter, and they immediately begin to explore the challenge and brainstorm potential solutions. They reach into the organization to conduct research, find data, and collect resources. As an executive team, we provided the challenge, but the teams were responsible for establishing the goal. They invariably set goals that were substantially more aggressive than either the team sponsor or I would have set. And yes, they almost always met those goals. It was interesting to watch folks who were new to an RA come into the room. They expressed disbelief that we could achieve the goals they set. By the end of the kick-off, they were ecstatic about how they could exceed it. This is the force multiplier effect that we came to rely on, and which ultimately changed the trajectory of the company.

The 90 days which followed the kick-off were intense. Teams were relentless in their pursuit of their goals. We remained available to advise, remove obstacles, and cheer them on. They worked tirelessly while also continuing to do their day jobs. Each team developed their own rhythm and approach. Some flew across the country for intense face-to-face sessions. They worked late into the evenings and on weekends. They reached out to the Volunteer Army for expertise and resources, and their original teams of 10-12 often swelled to 40-50 people by the time they were done. They also learned to not go down "rabbit holes" and also to pivot quickly when they needed to readjust.

We did full day check-ins at the 30- and 60-day marks. Not only did the teams work to solve the challenges with which they were presented, they were also responsible for making recommendations to sustain their work and integrate it back into the organization so they could successfully hand off their solutions. At the 90-day mark, we came back together so they could present their solutions. In addition to the executive team, we invited our senior leaders, the managers of the people who participated, our Kotter colleagues and the teams' "super volunteers" from the Volunteer Army. Dr. Kotter has also attended the occasional read-out. It was always a full house!

Teams presented their solutions with the same zeal and creativity with which they approached their challenge. No dry, boring PowerPoint presentations. We've seen teams create videos, music, innovative technologies, games, and other innovations to present their results. But it's not all sizzle with no steak. They presented deep and solid solutions with real value and incredibly significant dollars attached. Many senior executives attended these meetings to learn, ask questions, congratulate, and celebrate the success of these teams. This was critical to the success of our cultural journey. Employees at all levels interacted with executives, and having as many executives as possible "want to" attend was equally important.

The energy at these read-outs was astonishing. The teams always left exhausted but exhilarated. That exhilaration lasted for weeks. And then we would do it again. Interestingly, during COVID-19, we still held Results Accelerators and did all our work remotely, including the 30-day, 60-day, and final readouts. People were just as excited about presenting their findings and results remotely as they had been in person. Their presentations were equally creative and their results equally impressive. These enterprising teams made the best of it because they believed in the TBO and our mission.

There are many examples of the real results these teams produced, so I will share just a few. One RA team reduced product onboarding time by more than 60%—accelerating revenue and delighting customers. Another team was able to reduce more than 60% of their manual work by leveraging AI and Machine Learning.

These types of results required imagination and urgency; they resulted in real value.

THE GUIDING COALITION

 Dr. Kotter first talks about a Guiding Coalition in his 1996 book "Leading Change." It has become a critical part of his process for accelerating change.

A volunteer army needs a coalition of effective people— born of its own ranks—to guide, coordinate, and communicate its activities. Initially, our Urgency Team filled this role. But once that group had achieved its goal of enrolling 60% of the workforce in the Volunteer Army, their work was done. It was time to establish a new group to steward the Army, surround and support the Results Accelerators, and maintain urgency and commitment in the organization. This group would be known as the Guiding Coalition (GC).

A Guiding Coalition is made up of members who have sufficient influence, expertise, and credibility to drive change throughout the organization. This group must share high trust and team affinity, be emotionally committed to a successful implementation, and provide enough diversity of perspective and influence in the organization to offer well-rounded solutions and broad organizational impact. This must be a diverse group of leaders that represents all slices of the organization from top to bottom with a broad range of skills, connections, good reputations, leadership abilities, and management abilities. The group must also operate with urgency. The most important elements in a Guiding Coalition are diversity of the population (level, function, location, tenure, gender, etc.) and an ability to "leave the hierarchy behind" and work with people across all levels as respected peers.

Unlike the Urgency Team or the Results Accelerators, these team members are not hand-picked by leadership. Rather, employees apply for participation through a rigorous online application process (and this application system was created and maintained by employee volunteers). We typically received more than 100 applications for each year-long GC cycle.

The initial review of applications was done by a group of volunteers and executive leaders. The initial review was blinded, with no names or other distinguishing demographics revealed. This ensured that each application was considered and scored (by multiple reviewers) solely on the merit of its content. Only after the top candidates had been identified did we unblind the applications. This ensured appropriate diversity in terms of function, level, gender, race, and geographic location.

Each year, we selected approximately 50 people to join the Guiding Coalition. Each selectee makes a year-long commitment. In addition to the responsibilities outlined above, the GC also takes on their own initiatives. Ideas are pitched by the executive team (in a fun Shark Tank-like format) when the new GC first comes together. They can select from those pitched initiatives or select their own. Because their term is a year, GC initiatives tend to be more complex. They often have more of a cultural component than the Results Accelerators. If Results Accelerators represent the head of the organization, the GC represents the heart.

These initiatives could revolve around how to better connect remote employees (which proved to be invaluable when COVID demanded 100% work-from-home), improving the quality of our client deliverables, continuing to drive urgency, or nurturing and engaging the Volunteer Army. There were several additional goals designed to make HMS a better place to work or improve our performance and productivity.

HMS' Guiding Coalitions over the years left a lasting mark. They implemented Applause, a new recognition system, which allowed employees to recognize and reward each other. They implemented crucial new employee benefits—including maternity and paternity leave—and did so without increasing benefit costs. They designed and implemented Momentum, our first Customer Conference, which went on to become a hallmark of our organization (this was something we'd discussed for years, but it never happened until they made it happen). They conceived our first Hackathon, designed to identify and implement IT innovations.

Together, all of this summarizes the magic that Kotter brought to our organization. But as I watched it unfold, I quickly realized that the magic was in the people—and that Kotter's process simply helped us set our people free. And that we did. We made this process our own. And as our GC evolved over the years, we added many new paths toward urgency success.

Because Everything We Do Matters

P eople often ask me when I knew that we had captured the hearts of our workforce with this movement. The answer is easy. It was at the 90-day readout from our first round of Results Accelerators in 2016.

By then, the workforce was having a ball. They were energized, engaged, and having fun. We had critical mass enlisted in our Volunteer Army and lots of activity was occurring throughout the organization. But we hadn't yet produced business results to prove that this was more than an initiative to engage the workforce. Each of the five teams who participated in that first round produced astonishing results. But there was one team that captured both heads and hearts across the organization—and cemented this approach as part of the HMS culture.

This team was charged with driving revenue and engagement by better telling our story. The opportunity was described as follows:

> *We create profound impact for our clients and the people they serve; we typically FAR exceed our clients' expectations around ROI. But often they don't know the extent of this impact because ... we don't tell them, and we often don't share this internally with our HMS team either. We need to SING THIS FROM THE TALLEST TOWER!!!!! We need to be systematic around how we track and tell this story because we can immediately increase our profitability AND better understand the difference we make in people's lives as they navigate the complex health care system.*

The problem the team was trying to solve was this:

> *We do not regularly or proactively speak to the ROI we create, either with our clients or the greater HMS team. This is due to a variety of contributing factors including: lack of prioritization, no formal system of tracking and telling stories of impact, the siloed structure of our business, and a lack of concerted effort. We will change this, and we want to see BIG results that can SCALE.*

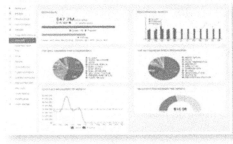

The Storytelling Team, which consisted of 15 people, decided to take a three-pronged approach. The first initiative in their solution was called "The Wall of Truth." This was to be a single source where frequently quoted value statistics could be housed for general access. This data would provide customers and HMS staff a real-time view of the value we had created in terms of dollars saved and payment recoveries for each of our customers. The team prioritized 25 metrics that could be manually compiled for this first version of the Wall of Truth, then they built an intranet site to package them (Keep in mind that they did not use traditional channels to do this work. The site wasn't built through our formal IT development process. It was built by excited volunteers who had the required skill set). They called this site HMS360—prong two of their approach.

With HMS360 in place, the team set out to provide proof of concept by selecting 15 clients with whom they would demo the product to test customer interest in this data. They were hoping to achieve overall satisfaction scores of 9 points or greater on a 10-point scale.

In four days, they created a demo of the new system and began flying across the country to share it with identified clients. Piling discretionary effort on top of discretionary effort, this team ultimately visited 16 customers across the country.

During each meeting, the team described their goals for this initiative, shared client-specific data, solicited feedback, and asked the client to evaluate the concept. They received valuable suggestions for improvement, which they used to update their approach after each visit. But the overall reaction was fabulous. Here are some customer comments:

> "Love the mobility of accessing our data whenever we need to."

> "No other vendor we work with understands our business the way HMS does."

> "We absolutely love it. Best tool we have seen, with detailed insights that are high value."

> "No other vendor has anything close."

We suddenly had a tool that helped our customers understand the value we were providing to them. We also had a way for our sales and service staff to tell our story more effectively. But did the average HMS employee fully understand the value of our work and the contribution they made to it? This team didn't think so. And their third prong aimed to address this.

 This strategy was called HMS Heartbeat. To begin, they identified three internal departments and engaged the leaders of those departments in helping to tell our story. They defined and documented the process by which each of these departments did their work. Next, they articulated how that work fit into the big picture to ultimately save and recover money for our customers, which could then be reallocated to benefit more people.

With these complex processes documented, they wrote video scripts and solicited volunteers to create clever, automated animations translating the complexities into easy-to-understand fundamentals. These animations articulated the value each of these departments were creating for our customers and those they served. They filmed the executive of each of these departments introducing the animations and thanking employees for their efforts. Finally, they held department meetings to present their package to the employees who made it all happen. The response was immediate and overwhelming. Some of the comments they received from our employees included:

> *"This was absolutely amazing. I did not realize how much it mattered what I do on a daily basis."*

> *"Thank you for allowing our team to be showcased and for us to feel important. I feel better as an employee and valued after watching the video."*

> *"I was unaware that the money we save for our clients actually does make its way back to the members."*

> *"This changes how I will go through my day."*

> *"It makes me want to work even harder for our members."*

Incredible! It was eye-opening for me too. The audience for these animations were the people who delivered value every day, but before this, they had never fully understood how their work contributed to HMS's success and the impact it had on people's lives. While this Results Accelerator team had completed these value packages for several departments (and had plans to do many more as part of their sustainability plan), they didn't want to end the project without giving every member of the HMS family that same experience. So, as their final project, they created the most heartwarming video I'd ever witnessed. It was to be distributed throughout the organization.

It was a simple video, again created completely by the team and their volunteers. It opened to a black screen, with white lettering and haunting music in the background. The words told the story of our work with New York's State Medicaid program.

In 2015, we recovered $475 million and saved an estimated $1.75 billion through prospective cost avoidance for New York Medicaid. The average cost of covering one person by New York Medicaid is $9,000. That means our recoveries may have enabled the program to cover an additional 53,000 people that year. *"That's a big, impersonal number,"* the words in the video went on to say, *"but what is personal—and what you may not know—is that some of those people are the children of your colleagues."* The video proceeded to tell the stories of 3 HMS employees who were also the parents of NY Medicaid recipients.

Those employees—those *parents*—all happened to be long-term HMS employees who had risen to senior levels of the organization. They were all well-known, respected, hard-charging, competent professionals. Through their willingness to reveal their very personal stories, they shared a vulnerability and courage that helped to underscore for their colleagues the value of their work. And in doing so, they touched the hearts of everyone who watched.

First, we met the irrepressible Matthew, a kindhearted 26-year-old man with autism. Through New York's Medicaid Waiver program, Matthew was able to live in a group home with wonderful caregivers, work at a job, and even, he told us with excitement, go to camp each summer. His mom's eyes shone with tears as she explained the relief she felt that Matthew could stay in a wonderful, multigenerational setting where she knew he would be cared for.

Next, we were introduced to 8-year-old Sammy. A twin, Sammy was born prematurely at 28 weeks. A brain hemorrhage shortly after her birth left her battling cerebral palsy, epilepsy, and encephalitis. Through the video, we were given the privilege of watching this curly-haired cherub grow, alongside her healthy twin, from a baby to the young lady she is today. Her therapies were expensive, her mom explained, and would not have been possible without support from New York's Medicaid Waiver program. At the end of her video, we watched Sammy smiling as she ran toward the camera.

Finally, we met Keegan, another 8-year-old. Keegan has cerebral palsy; he is non-verbal and non-ambulatory. After leaning over to gently kiss Keegan's forehead, his mother described the support and services he received through New York's Medicaid Waiver program. These services provide him with a richness of life and experiences he would not otherwise have.

The love and pride each mother felt shone through in their stories. Each looked directly into the camera and provided heartfelt thanks to their colleagues for their work, support, and impact.

One mom summed up the sentiments for all of them when she said, "I thank each and every one of you at HMS—my friends, my colleagues—for what you do to help save money for the New York Medicaid program. If you ever wonder if what you do every day makes a difference in people's lives, I would ask you to think about my child and others like him, and realize that what you do enables parents like me to sleep better at night. So, on behalf of me, my family, and parents of all the other amazing children that are served under Medicaid by New York's Developmental Disability waiver, my sincere thanks."

As you might imagine, there wasn't a dry eye in the house as this Results Accelerators team concluded their final readout. I still watch this video to remind myself of the real impact of our work, and of how we make a difference in people's lives. And yes, I still shed tears of joy for these strong mothers who work more than a full-time job, and who were so willing to take the time to tell their stories. I have a profound, everlasting respect for each of them.

Remember, all these results were delivered by 15 people in 90 days, while each continued to perform their day jobs. Sounds impossible, right? That's the point. These people performed because they *wanted* to—not because they *had* to. And they didn't rely only on the 15 members of the original team. They reached deep into the organization and engaged hundreds of people in pursuit of their goals. The team leader and executive sponsor didn't lead this initiative with detailed project plans, controls, and assignments. They led by providing a vision and encouraging the team to go where that vision led them. They provided support and encouragement, and they helped them remove roadblocks and overcome setbacks. They didn't manage. They led.

This was just one of five teams that participated in that first round of Results Accelerators. I could tell equally inspiring stories about any one of the others—the journey they took, the results they produced, the impact they had. But I chose this one because that was the moment our workforce *truly* realized what we were doing was different—and our culture was here to stay.

The impact of the Storytelling Team's work continues to resonate today. The tagline they used in their animations and video "Because Everything We Do Matters" took off within the workforce. People began adding it to the bottom of their email signatures. They ordered logo shirts for team recognition events with these words proudly printed on them. You may have noticed that the words appear at the bottom of our Big Opportunity statement. They were not part of our original statement—they were added when we revised the statement because of what they meant to our employees.

 Most importantly, our workforce began to calculate the impact of the savings and recoveries they were delivering to our customers and translating those into the value they created. One team estimated the number of children who could receive health care coverage based on the savings they generated. They created a handprint for each of these children and decorated their offices with them. What an impressive and inspirational visual reminder of the differences they make!

Nothing made me prouder than knowing that the HMS family deeply understood that everything they do matters. Because it does!

The Payoff

From the beginning, I've said that this work was not an employee engagement initiative. Our goal—and a foundation of my entire career—was to create an environment where all people could contribute to their fullest ability, where everyone performed with purpose and passion, and where our work was about doing good while also taking care of ourselves. I wanted us to be unwavering in our service to customers and shareholders. Above all else, I wanted us to contribute to serving others.

There are many metrics that can be used to measure the value of these goals and the effectiveness of our TBO effort, and we used all of them. But before we dive into those quantifiable metrics, I want to share a story that underscored, for me, the culture change this work drove.

RESULTS IN ACTION

2020 kicked off full of promise. Our full-year 2019 numbers showed solid revenue and profit. Revenue increased 4.7%, net income rose 58.5%, and adjusted EBITDA increased 10.6% from the prior year, and we had record operating cash flow performance. We entered 2020 with optimism that we would continue to experience top- and bottom-line growth driven by product innovation, entry into new markets, application of new technologies, and expansion with both current and new clients.

We expected our growth in 2020 to be fueled by investments in sales talent, technology, data analytics, and product development and the strategic acquisitions we had completed in the prior year. As we flipped the calendar from 2019 to 2020, we had full schedules and high expectations it would be our best year ever.

Then … the world shut down!

We'd heard of the novel coronavirus that was wreaking havoc overseas, but we expected it would be contained before it reached our shores. Even when the first US case was confirmed in late January, reassured by our federal government, we continued to hope for the best.

In early March, we brought our salesforce together in Arizona for several days of training and awards. On the trip home, we began to feel more uneasy. We were seeing masks in airports and hearing reports of increasing cases and deaths. And the CDC said we were heading for a pandemic.

I had just returned from Australia, a new market for us that we'd been cultivating. The opportunities for HMS in that nation were further clarified while I was there, and we were excited about capitalizing on those opportunities in 2020. Pretty soon, everything was flipped on its head.

On March 11th, days after the HMS Sales team returned from Arizona and I returned from Australia, the World Health Organization declared COVID-19 a pandemic.

If there was one thing we learned from our TBO initiative, it was urgency—and that urgency kicked in immediately. Our Chief Medical Officer took the lead in providing guidance, information, and policy. While we always had about one third of our workforce who worked from home, this crisis meant we had to pivot and enable all employees to work remotely. They needed all the equipment, technologies, and training necessary to continue serving our customers. We had just acquired a new company in December and had to move all these new employees to work from home as well. This was a group for whom that concept was completely foreign. This process included leasing, loading our software, and deploying 700 new laptops!

And yet, we accomplished it all within about two weeks! I credit this to the urgency, volunteerism, and sense of community our employees and leaders felt. Had this happened five years ago, we would have not recovered so quickly.

But the workforce was frightened. We all were. This was unprecedented. Our cities and towns were closed and our children were home from school. Grocery stores were empty. People were starting to die from COVID-19. And no one could tell us how long it would last.

That's the void that our workforce decided—on their own—to step into. Our Guiding Coalition wanted to make a difference in the lives of their colleagues during this crisis, so they pulled together (virtually) and created a plan. Within one week, they had developed and tested a comprehensive website—called "In This Together"—that people could access from any electronic device. It featured an area for our Chief Medical Officer to provide medical information and corporate updates. They shared tips and training for remote working and home schooling. They provided information relating to food insecurity. There was a section called "What's Cooking" for employees to share recipes and pictures of their quarantine meals. There was a list of links and activities designed to engage school-age children while parents were working. They contacted a former executive and licensed yoga instructor and asked her to provide online yoga sessions for the workforce. The mom of one of our employees is a professional therapist, and she graciously provided videos on stress and anxiety reduction.

Simultaneously, our Guiding Coalition began releasing a series of videos called "Working at Home." Several times a week, they would feature a colleague sharing his or her "new normal." Our employees showed us their workspace, introduced us to their new coworkers (children, spouses, and pets), and gave us a peek into their lives during that crazy, frightening time. These videos were fun, funny, and wildly popular. Executives would release regular updates via video—either me or another member of the executive leadership team. This practice brought everyone closer as we fought the dreariness of quarantine together.

The workforce supported each other in so many ways throughout the crisis. It wasn't just our human resources department worrying about the morale of the workforce—it was every employee, in it together. They understood the struggles of balancing work and homeschooling, the blurred lines between work and life, and the challenges of two working spouses and online schooling happening simultaneously. Heck, they were even mailing toilet paper across the country to help weather the shortages we were facing.

If ever there was a situation that could be described as a burning platform, COVID-19 was it. But our workforce framed it through a different, more optimistic lens—as an opportunity they had to bring together their colleagues from across the country. They could create an environment where everyone could continue to thrive, and where we could ensure our customers remained at the center of everything. I could not be prouder of the entire HMS team.

When I look from my heart, it's *those* results that jump out. There is no doubt that a fully engaged workforce who believe in their ability to create nearly impossible results can move mountains. And this team did. We didn't miss a beat—even in the earliest days of the pandemic.

QUANTITATIVE RESULTS

There are plenty of success metrics to prove our case from those who operate primarily from the head. These people are only convinced by tangible results.

From 2014 to 2020, we saw a 53% increase in revenue, an 82% jump in AEBITDA, and a significant stock price surge from $8.84 a share to $37—all while retaining 97% of top talent and a 91% Glassdoor CEO approval rating.

Over the same period, employee engagement soared from 61.7% to 82.8%. Manager effectiveness increased to 89%.

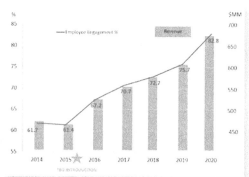

Many of these indicators are lagging so we also paid close attention to leading indicators throughout our journey. The trajectory was not always a straight line trending upwards, but any downward trends we saw were quickly corrected. Since we had implemented better management information controls, we were also able to share a much deeper level of metrics with our workforce, and we found that it was information they were hungry for. With data at their fingertips, they were able to take quick action to analyze and address gaps in our results.

I remember one particularly disappointing quarter. It was the 3rd quarter of 2018, and our results had failed to match our expectations. All our leading indicators were trending upwards, and it was discouraging to see financial results lag. Due to the complexity of our work, our revenue could be "lumpy" on a quarterly basis – and that could be an irritant to public shareholders.

Our Organizational Development team was scheduled for their quarterly strategy meeting with our Kotter team at their headquarters in Cambridge, MA, and our financial lagging was specifically what they wanted to address. They drew all the levers of success we were measuring on the giant whiteboard wall in the Kotter conference room. Each lever showed an upward trend. Given these results, they asked Dr. Kotter, "Why aren't we seeing the corresponding increase in revenue that all your research suggested we should expect?"

Dr. Kotter didn't miss a beat. Jumping right into professorial mode, he grabbed a marker and approached the whiteboard. "There could be three reasons," he explained, "why we were not seeing the financial results we wanted." They were:

1. We may have missed an important lever and were not measuring everything that was relevant to achieving results. The team discussed this intensively and agreed that was likely not the cause.
2. Market conditions were such that the level of results we were achieving were reasonable and were outpacing our peers in this market space. We knew that was not the case.
3. We hadn't given it enough time since financial indicators will always lag cultural indicators, and it might take another quarter or two for financial results to catch up.

The team agreed they could be patient for a while longer. And just one quarter later, we began to see—and sustain—the growth we had set as our goal. It didn't happen overnight, but it did happen quickly. It was clear: the work we'd put in to build a high-performing culture—and the magic that the Kotter approach brought to us (which we ultimately made our own)—was at the heart of our success.

THE IMPACT ON EMPLOYEES

It would be impossible to talk about the pay-off from our cultural journey without talking about the impact it had on our workforce. In the early days at HMS, I knew most everyone by name. As our geographic spread increased and our workforce grew to over 3,000 people, I no longer knew them all. I found myself relying on a smaller group of "go-to" people to get things done. Yet my travels throughout the nation convinced me there was plenty of untapped potential out there—but we had to unleash it.

The outpouring of energy that occurred when we introduced TBO was immediate and astonishing. Within days, it became clear we had thousands of people who desperately wanted to make a bigger contribution. It was one of the great joys of my career to watch our employees, from every function, every level, and every corner of the United States (and ultimately Australia and India) grow, learn, and contribute. Our cultural work transformed a big company into a tight-knit family. In my final days as CEO, I knew most of our employees and they knew me—and they knew each other. They wouldn't hesitate to drop me a note or pick up the phone to make suggestions, seek help, or ask me to help them overcome obstacles. They knew it was safe to reach out to the CEO or respond honestly to one of my blogs.

While achieving our financial goals took some time, the impact on the workforce was immediate. Almost instantly, we saw a sharp reduction in voluntary regrettable turnover, which continued quarter after quarter. As we uncovered talent deep within our organization, we were able to fill leadership positions internally much more frequently than we had in the past. Our employee engagement scores soared in the first year after we engaged Kotter, then continued improving every year since. We also added one question to our survey that first year: "Are you in the Volunteer Army?" We discovered that engagement for employees who were part of the HMS Volunteer Army scored almost ten points higher in their first year, and that trend has proven true every year since. Clearly, people wanted to contribute to a purpose that was bigger than their day-to-day work. We'd tapped into the human spirit.

And our workforce communicated how they felt about our cultural journey. Each year, we receive thousands of comments during our annual "Voice of the Employee" engagement survey. This survey is taken extremely seriously by executives and the workforce. We generally see a participation rate of 90% or greater. Employee input guides our business plans and engagement actions. My executive team and I would read every comment, then act on them. I've pulled some representative comments from our most recent survey to give you a flavor for how our employees feel about the journey we were on together:

> "I appreciate what the company does overall, by helping to save billions of healthcare dollars. The ability to see how different departmental job functions influence this is inspiring and what makes me proud to work at HMS."

> "All of the videos and things I have seen since we have joined with HMS have been nothing less than inspiring. Hearing high ups in a company talk to people on a human level and talk about working with your heads and your hearts. Not always just talking about the money and making money. Everyone wants to make money but to hear how to help people and make a difference is inspiring. I'm so excited and proud to join in with HMS and hope that I have great things on my horizon."

> "The day I watched Bill Lucia get up in front of the entire team and truly and emotionally deliver a speech on what racial and social division does to people. He wasn't just a CEO professing a corporate ethos, but a human sharing his heart. Of all the things I struggle with in a company, I have not once doubted the truth that who we are based on heritage, identity or belief adds to us as a group. I have shared that experience with many people who have looked for employment. I want to see HMS succeed because the world is better with people who think that way."

> "Head and heart... we walk the walk. I really believe it is part of our DNA."

> "I love the passion, honesty, and 'team player' sense I get from senior mgmt. This is the first place I've worked that I feel like I could actually have lunch with any of them."

"The integrity and high moral compass of upper management. The inclusivity of the success of the company and what seems to drive decisions and the actions of our company, internally and externally. I honestly believe that upper management leads with their head AND heart."

"I am proud of HMS & love working at HMS because at the end of each day, I walk away smiling because I know our actions—individually and as a team—make a positive difference in the world and for the lives that we touch."

I may have gotten a bit carried away with the number of examples I selected, but honestly, there are hundreds more just like them to choose from. What comes through most for me is the consistency of the language they use. They *so clearly* understand the social significance of their work, and they feel impassioned and empowered to contribute.

EMPLOYEE TESTIMONIALS

 We reached out to ask some employees if they would tell their stories about how this cultural journey has impacted their lives and their careers. First up is Joseph Sforza. Joseph is a Senior Director in Operations in our Dallas office. Here is what Joe had to say:

"My writing could never do TBO and its impact on me justice. First, let me say—I'm enterally in debt to those who made this possible at HMS. You changed my life for the better. Pushed me further than I thought I could go. Celebrated my wins and helped me tease out lessons learned from the low points. I'll keep the head and heart lessons with me always.

I went from volunteering to edit videos via a TBO request to leading multiple Result Accelerators across our largest products. Throughout the journey, I learned the power of leading from the head AND HEART. Admittedly, the heart portion of my leadership style was lacking when I started my TBO journey. After editing the HMS heartbeat video and seeing it's impact on our culture, I learned you can move so many more people when you incorporate both head and heart. For me, it marked the first time I ever felt connected to the work I did. Prior to that, I did not know that every dollar of revenue we generated created x10 return for Medicaid programs. Those dollars went to taking care of the most in need in our society."

 Alexa Crenshaw was a Program Director in our Government Account Management department and a former co-lead of our Guiding Coalition 3.0. Here is what Alexa shared:

"TBO has significantly impacted my career and how I view leadership. It has changed everything for me and sculpted who I have become as an employee, manager, and person. Leading from the heart is not only something I practice at work, but it has also bled into my personal life. Because of TBO, I enjoy what I do—which in turn helps me be a better wife, mother, and friend.

My involvement in TBO occurred by happenstance. Prior to getting involved, I spent months wondering if I should leave the company and find a place that valued my contributions. One day, a Senior Manager who I had grown close with reached out to me and recommended that I apply for the Guiding Coalition (GC). I had no idea what was in store for me. After attending the first sessions of GC, the energy was electric—I completely "bought in" to the idea of TBO and thrived off the optimism and feeling of belonging. There were no titles, no power trips—each member of that group felt as if they were part of something bigger and something that truly made a difference. Shortly after joining the Guiding Coalition, I chose to volunteer for a group whose mission was to collect and share stories. The Heartbeat Storytelling team opened my eyes to what I was missing. It wasn't until I heard others' stories that I realized I was right in the middle of creating my own. I found myself getting emotional— hearing stories opened my eyes to the incredible success of the company I work for. From there, TBO culture was engrained into everything that I do.

Getting involved in TBO opened many doors for me. I became a leader. I was seen and respected, and most importantly, I felt that my work was valued. Not only did the leadership opportunities through TBO hone my existing skills, but it also allowed me to shine in my day-to-day role, which led to an internal promotion. In the midst of what felt like craziness during my day-to-day role, the little reprieve I found was volunteering for activities through TBO. Those activities showed me that I was making an impact and in turn allowed me to love my day job. My monotonous job turned into a love for my career and a true passion for helping others. In the four years I have been involved with TBO, I have been approached by many outside opportunities—but none of them measured up to the feeling of impact and accomplishment that I get at this company. The culture is unmatched, and I have felt true belonging here at HMS."

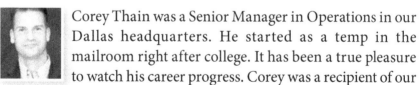 Corey Thain was a Senior Manager in Operations in our Dallas headquarters. He started as a temp in the mailroom right after college. It has been a true pleasure to watch his career progress. Corey was a recipient of our prestigious Galen Powers Award, in which the HMS Board of Directors recognized an outstanding individual whose superb work has impacted the organization. This award is also a testament to their commitment to ethic, quality, and compliance, and how the recipient improved HMS's performance for clients and the people they serve. Corey was involved in TBO since the original Urgency Team that kicked it all off. He's served in one role or another ever since. Here is what Corey had to say:

"Through TBO, HMS turned away from mediocre corporate culture and instead embraced a way of thinking that has brought everyone together to achieve common goals. People of all backgrounds, personalities, and titles work together voluntarily on projects that better the healthcare system and give back to our communities. When you work with someone who truly believes in leading from the heart and finding the 'want to' in what they do, you cannot help but want to join in. Through TBO, my HMS career launched, and it has allowed me to develop skills that I never would have imagined. Because of TBO, I love what I do, and I see the value in my role every single day.

Personally, TBO has really helped me build confidence in myself and, more importantly, in others. I now see the best in everyone regardless of preconceived notions, title, or experience. I believe that anything is achievable—with hard work and determination, you can accomplish what you set your mind to if you work together on something that everyone involved is passionate about.

Professionally, TBO has enabled me to grow as a leader and has really taught me to never underestimate the power of a passionate group of people.

I have been with HMS for 18 years. Before TBO, I was in a lower-level position in the mail room, as a Team Lead in Operations. I felt stuck in a dead-end job, and change didn't seem to be in my future. I had always pushed for continuous improvement and change, but I had limited support and very limited exposure to Senior Leadership. TBO changed all of that. I am now a Senior Manager in Operations and have changed roles multiple times since the introduction of The Big Opportunity at HMS.

Titles mean nothing in TBO—everyone comes in as equals regardless of your day job. You have access to a Volunteer

Army of your peers to support you and executive leadership to assist and guide you in your mission. TBO allowed me to take part in exciting strategic initiatives—which would have been seemingly impossible to conquer on my own yet were now achievable with the help of the TBO volunteer army.

If I were to sum it up in a few sentences, TBO changed the culture in a very positive way at HMS. It made work FUN, challenging, and exciting. TBO gave those involved something different to look forward to every day and allowed them to connect with some really smart people they would have never met in their day job. Reflecting on the past five years and talking with team members, everyone agrees the CONNECTIONS that are made have the most impact. The connections with people and the relationships built working on TBO initiatives is what really improved the culture. It made a company with thousands of employees feel like one big family. All employees feel connected and in touch with the same mission: improving the healthcare system and making HMS a great company to work for."

 Kelly Ruiz was a Project Manager for our Eligibility group. She works remotely from Kentucky. Kelly was an active volunteer before being selected as a GC co-lead. Here is Kelly's story:

"TBO changed HMS by leaps and bounds. TBO has given normal employees like me a place to feel like a leader. No longer having to ask for permission and the freedom to fail fast and pivot if we needed to t complete our goals. The changes in the last five years are profound. It makes my heart so happy to know that this story—a story of love and success—is going to be told!

TBO has provided an accessible way for me to knock on doors and see which of them open. Not all of them do, but certainly more of them have opened for me than if I'd not been able to knock at all.

Some opportunities that have presented themselves to me during my time in the TBO are:

- *Networking galore. I know and have meaningful relationships with colleagues nationwide. Prior to TBO, my world was limited to my virtual interactions with a small office in Indiana.*
- *An expanded product knowledge. As you get to know the people, you intrinsically learn more about what each of them does.*
- *The opportunity to head a team that is leading a global corporate initiative like the Hackathon series.*
- *Direct career strategy suggestions. Recently, a VP mentioned my name to a hiring manager in another department. I am certain that my name would have not come to mind without the exposure I gained from my work with TBO and the Guiding Coalition. I am currently interviewing for that position to expand my career footprint and continue to make my work matter.*
- *Camaraderie. I thoroughly enjoy the time spent with my expanded network of coworkers. It's not simply a career strategy, it actually makes the day-to-day more enjoyable.*

TBO shows HMS employees that they are valued as the company's greatest resource. Instead of hiring consultants, HMS often looks inward to solve issues and trends. Not only does this save money, it demonstrates that the Executive Leadership Team trusts its own team to get the job done right. It's empowering."

Finally, we have Reginald Vincent. Reg was also involved in TBO since the very beginning. Not only did he prove to be an avid volunteer and leader, but he is also a true student of the craft. Here are Reg's reflections on our journey:

"I became an engineer because I love to build, and the TBO journey helped me learn how to build an urgent, empowered organization. Culture is the combination of actions and attitudes, and our leadership team championed our change at the highest level. From the start of the journey until now, the relentless focus from the leadership team to drive that culture has been evident in the success of urgency.

The major moment for me was the ideation, development, and revealing of HMS360 (a client portfolio product) to the company. It taught me firsthand how user-centered design happens in practice and how it works. We met the customer at their site, showed them how we built the prototype in four days with their data, described the challenges and successes, and revealed the beta product. 'I'd like to use this with my other vendors,' was one response, followed by several similar questions and requests. That moment, and many others (including showing the product to our Board of Directors) shows the power of using urgency, crowdsourcing, and innovation methods to drive customer satisfaction.

I have always been urgent—it's in my DNA—but TBO has changed my approach on how to scale urgency. Now, I take every moment to drive urgency culture in every opportunity that I have before me. It has also helped me become a better leader, coach, mentor, and teammate. I thank our leaders, volunteers, and champions—both past and present—for driving, supporting, and building an innovative culture at HMS."

These five employees are representatives of the talent, passion, and heart of the HMS workforce. Their thoughtful reflections fill me with gratitude and pride. They thank *me* for providing these opportunities. But I never forget for one moment that it is *me* who must thank *them*. My greatest honor in life has been to lead this amazing company and the very dedicated and passionate employees. It has been a privilege to watch this workforce soar to such heights. The greatest payoff of this journey is the difference the HMS workforce has made in the world.

The Price of Success
is Eternal Vigilance

The state of our culture was strong in 2017. We could not have been prouder. But we also began to realize that sustaining the energy and passion that was driving this culture would require more than just staying on the same path.

Let's face it: Disney World is a magical place, but if you go every day, it eventually becomes routine. The same was true of our cultural journey. As exciting as each part of our TBO effort was, as we moved into rounds 4 and 5 of our Guiding Coalition, or rounds 9 and 10 of our Results Accelerators, we risked these things becoming just a routine part of how we did business. While this might have proven that we'd successfully integrated these practices into our business, we also wanted to keep the sense of adventure and wonder alive in the workforce. We began to innovate early in the process.

SUSTAINING ACCELERATORS

Our first big innovation was the brainchild of Doug Williams (our Executive Vice President) and Jimmy Leppert (our Kotter associate). Doug had recently taken on responsibility for our Program Integrity business, and he was laser-focused on increasing process efficiency and yield. He had sponsored a couple of Results Accelerators in the first rounds of that effort, with great results. However, Doug noticed that as the teams solved one issue as a part of a Results Accelerator, they invariably broke something else, either upstream or downstream from the process step on which they had been working. He began to envision a series of initiatives divided into 90-day sprints (just like an RA) but which connected as part of the end-to-end process. Rather than pulling people from their day jobs into cross functional teams, he believed these should be staffed by people *as part of* their day jobs—and that each team should include everyone involved with any part of the process they wanted to improve. Thus, the Sustaining Accelerators were born.

There were many learnings along the way—chief among them the importance of building these teams into cohesive groups equally committed to achieving the outcomes they had established for themselves. Like many companies, our teams tended to operate in silos. The problem with that is that each team tends to want to optimize their own results, even if comes at the expense of other functions. Seeing as our approach was to achieve maximum results, this invariably led to tensions that had to be resolved.

We borrowed many of the techniques we had been using to build executive health within the executive leadership team. The Sustaining Accelerator teams completed DiSC profiles and EQi assessments, and we brought in our executive coach, Debjani Biswas, to help them better understand themselves and each other. Perhaps most importantly, we aligned the reinforcers that drove each group to support the overall success of the end-to-end process. Those actions proved to be the big differentiator. They helped these teams to coalesce toward a common goal.

Our Sustaining Accelerators proved to be successful beyond our wildest dreams. Doug summed it up when he said, "As a result of multiple acquisitions that were not fully integrated, our Payment Integrity assets were not working in tandem. When we began to attack all the parts of the broken system—and do it in a coordinated, focused way with the energy of many, many people—that's when we multiplied our performance." Some of the results we saw included reduced contract to recovery time (inaccurate payments recovered on behalf of our clients) by 59%; our quality and process improvements raised the monthly medical record request rate by 83%; using natural language processing and AI reduced manual reviews by 63%; and turnaround times were reduced by 29%. These results proved to us that we could build new tools alongside our Kotter colleagues *and* on our own, which our employees were hungry for.

INTEGRATION ACCELERATORS

Another challenge on our journey was to integrate new people into the fold, especially those who had not been with us from the beginning. Early on, the Guiding Coalition integrated TBO into our new hire orientation program and regularly invited new employees to join the Volunteer Army and become part of action teams throughout the organization. This effort was successful, and we were able to sustain participation at nearly 60% of the organization throughout the journey. Our real challenge—since we were in a heavy acquisition period and doing so was consistent with our strategy—was to engage companies that joined us via acquisition.

According to collated research and a recent Harvard Business Review report, the failure rate for mergers and acquisitions sits between 70% and 90%. Deloitte asserts that culture has emerged as one of the dominant barriers to effective integrations. We agree. We believe effective cultural integration is important to achieving the anticipated synergies that drive acquisitions. It was important to our Board of Directors and to our shareholders. Thus, for us, effective integration became a business imperative, and we were convinced that what we had learned in building our own culture could be leveraged to accelerate a successful integration.

In 2017, we acquired the Eliza Corporation, headquartered in Danvers, Massachusetts. This was our largest acquisition since our TBO effort began. We felt very ready to receive them. The Guiding Coalition took the lead on creating a welcome strategy. They enlisted the HMS workforce to write individual, hand-written notes welcoming Eliza employees to the HMS family, put together welcome packages, distributed Kotter's book "That's Not How We Do It Here," and created an urgency team at Eliza to help engage the Eliza workforce in our big opportunity. We expected a smooth, accelerated integration.

We couldn't have been more wrong.

We underestimated the loss the Eliza workforce was feeling. They were suspicious of our motives. They misinterpreted our outreach. They railed against changes to practices and policies. And they had NO interest in our Big Opportunity.

In retrospect, we should have anticipated all of this. But we were learning too. What we did do was to stay the course. We listened to them. We rectified some things that they saw as substantial takeaways (such as a popular health plan option that was not part of our benefits package). And we continued to work with the Eliza Urgency team, which was made up of influential thought leaders who'd been hand-selected by Eliza's executive team. The breakthrough came about six months into the integration, when it suddenly dawned on us that our mistake was in trying to engage them in *our* big opportunity. They had no connection to it—they hadn't participated in its creation, and they had substantial loyalty to their own mission. Voila! That unlocked the magic. We brought our two missions together with our Big Opportunity, and we asked this simple question:

"What is possible tomorrow that wasn't possible yesterday?"

They immediately began to see the benefits of our greater resources and reach for achieving the mission about which they were so passionate. From that moment on, they were onboard. By engaging senior leaders from both companies in Integration Accelerators, quickly became engaged in positive action together. Former Eliza employees have since become some of our greatest champions. Lisa Freeman Foote was a Director in our Health Engagement Design team in the Danvers office. Here is what she had to say:

> *"TBO has changed me, which changed my team and ultimately impacted HMS as a whole. What I mean is that it's helped me explore the way I lead the team and how to allow others to pursue their interests outside of their regular day job. And because there is this freedom (and support), HMS benefited too. More and more people began to demonstrate passion and excitement around everything we did.*

When you see your CEO and other leaders acting as 'real' people—not as traditional 'business' people—it changes you and the way you think about your role and the entire company. I've had several leaders (formal managers and otherwise) in my career, and each of them has taught me something about the best way to lead a team. But nothing has been more impactful than seeing the TBO in action. It took a while for it to click with me, but once it did, I realized that each of the four principles are not meant to be treated individually. When combined, that's when the magic happens.

Do I know the TBO principles? Yes. Can I recite them? Yes. Do I need to preach them to everyone willing to listen? No. Simply by acting and living them each day, people I interact with learn and eventually adopt them too. I've stopped calling on just a few senior folks on my team to do all the projects. Everyone has unique skills, hence why they were hired originally, and as a leader I needed to change the status quo and allow others to use their skills or learn new skills. When I call on the many, it's a success. A 'have to' attitude exists when there is no trust among team members and leadership that things will be done (and done right). Flip this on its head and empower people, and they'll step up. Why? Because empowerment is a powerful tool that makes people feel good about what they are contributing. When they 'want to' do things, that's a success. Your heart is a powerful tool when it comes to business. That's often forgotten.

Once people are enabled and set free, you can learn so much more about them and their motivations. And it's amazing to see them blossom and grow. That's when an unstoppable sustainable environment is formed—because everyone is thinking 'we are in this together.'"

I had the great opportunity to speak with Lisa well after HMS was sold. She now has a new career and a role in the cultural transformation team at Gainwell Technologies. That's how impactful this work was to her.

Our experience with Eliza prepared us with far more powerful tools when we acquired Accent, a payment accuracy and cost containment business, in late 2019. Armed with the lessons from Eliza, our initial approach was much more nuanced and sensitive. We took the time to listen before we engaged by conducting listening tours with the employees immediately after the close. We created a shared Big Opportunity based on the synergies we both believed we could achieve. And we formed teams—comprised of both Accent and HMS employees—to work on projects that would have the most substantial impact on achieving the synergies of the integration. Called Integration Accelerators, these 90-day projects served to accelerate business results and bring teams together in a deeper and more meaningful way as they worked together to realize the promise of the integration. Here is what one of our new former Accent employees had to say:

> *"I feel since joining this company that from top to bottom people really believe in leading with the head and heart and that it's not just about numbers but improving our customers' quality of life and doing what's right. That makes me want to get up and come to work each day."*

The Accent integration was honestly one of the smoothest I've ever experienced. There were few missteps, Accent was integrated seamlessly, and we began to see return on investment very quickly. Based on these innovations, Integration Accelerators have become part of our repertoire.

FAST TRACKS

Fast Tracks was another innovation we invented to pursue further success and keep things fresh. Unlike Results Accelerators, which focused on a strategically important issue on which progress could be achieved in 90 days, Fast Tracks tend to be more grassroots. The team self-selects, sets their own time frame, and establishes their goals. Managers can identify a Fast Track within their own department, and employees can pull a group together, seek an Executive Sponsor, and identify the problem they want to solve. Fast Tracks expanded ownership throughout the organization and made it possible for many more initiatives to be underway simultaneously.

CULTURAL IMMERSION

Effectively integrating newly hired and acquired employees into our culture wasn't the only challenge we faced. Executives come and go. As we acquired new businesses, we also acquired new senior leaders and executives. There's no doubt that the active engagement and support of the executive team is a pivotal part of the success we have seen, so it was imperative that we brought this group of people on board quickly and sincerely.

We started that process before we brought new executives on board. Our commitment to this cultural journey was introduced during the interview process. We shared the process and the principles and outlined our results. We selected our most zealous champions from throughout the workforce to participate in the interview processes. We gauged potential new executive reactions and evaluated the stories they told about the cultures in which they had worked. Most importantly, we made it clear that support of this effort by the executive team was the one thing in this company that is a "*have to*" and not a "*want to.*"

Once a new executive or senior leader came on board, we put them through an intense cultural immersion program. We partnered them with a senior level champion and a Kotter partner to guide them in the early days of their own journey. We assigned them to a project

(RA sponsor or team leader; GC sponsor, etc.) as quickly as feasible, alongside a seasoned executive sponsor. We coached them along the way and cheered on their results. As they created their own nearly impossible results through these teams, we watched them become true owners of our high-performing culture.

NETWORK OF COACHES

Another brilliant innovation I'm proud of is the creation of a network of internal coaches to support the workforce. This came about because veterans of Results Accelerators and the Guiding Coalition found they did not want to step away once their commitment was over. These tended to be people who were profoundly changed by their experience. They brought skills and wisdom to the process and possessed deep learnings of TBO lessons.

As our program grew and we added new innovations to the process, our internal Organizational Development team was stretched thin. So, this was a perfect solution. In partnership with our Kotter colleagues, we built intense training regimens to school these folks in back-of-the-house techniques required to create the magic.

Today, HMS assigns a coach to every Guiding Coalition sub-team, Results Accelerator, Sustaining Accelerator, or Integration Accelerator team. Coaches provide invaluable insights to the teams and their leaders. In doing so, they exponentially increase the depth of knowledge and commitment.

BY PEOPLE AND BY SYSTEMS

As we consider the things an organization must do to sustain cultural success, let's revisit our behavioral definition of culture.

Culture is the pattern of behaviors that are reinforced by people and by systems over time. Much of this book has highlighted the people-reinforcement approaches we deployed to bring our high-performing culture to life. But it is equally important to make sure your systems are also aligned to reinforce the behaviors you espouse, and we also spend a great deal of time on this.

Earlier, I discussed how we redesigned our financial and management information systems to drive the new behaviors that were required to fuel our success. Now, let me turn our attention to the ways in which we redesigned our human capital systems.

One of the tools our internal team used to diagnose and assess people-related organizational issues is called "The Levers of Human Performance." This instrument, and the tools that support it, allow our team to assess those aspects that most impact performance and the interrelationships between them. That allows them to take a multidisciplinary approach to interventions designed to improve people's performance.

Many of these levers have systems associated with them, which we took careful consideration in crafting. Our staffing systems have been aligned to ensure that we are sourcing and hiring people with the skills and attitudes that drive our success. We have adopted a behavioral, team-based approach to interviewing and hiring. New employee onboarding and orientation have been redesigned, and we made substantial changes to align our organizations and the jobs within them.

Our most recent alignment effort focused on performance management and compensation systems. We came to believe that our traditional annual performance management process did not support the agile, urgent culture we wanted to sustain. It did not drive valuable performance dialogue between manager and employee; it did not allow for goal adjustment as priorities shifted; it did not easily integrate third party feedback; and it drove too much focus on annual ratings.

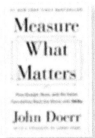

We ultimately selected a new system based on OKRs (Objectives and Key Results) based on the work of John Doerr and Larry Page in their book "Measure What Matters."[12]

Our new system is a collaborative goal-setting tool. It allows employees and their managers to set challenging, ambitious goals with measurable results. OKRs allow employees to track progress, create alignment, and encourage engagement around measurable goals. Rather than an annual exercise, we set OKRs quarterly in interactive discussions between managers and employees, and we also evaluate progress each quarter. A simple star system replaces the annual numeric performance rating. It is simple and streamlined, and it drives the behaviors we want in the organization.

At the same time, we redesigned our compensation systems and processes to ensure a better alignment between performance and pay. We had long rewarded performance based on both what the employee achieved and how they achieved it—to drive a value and values-based culture. With our redesigned performance management system, we also wanted to ensure employees were being rewarded based on both their performance in their day jobs and the discretionary efforts they were applying to other projects and volunteer activities.

I cannot overstate how important this is: ensure that your systems reinforce the cultural behaviors you are trying to drive. Too often, an organization will tell you they expect certain things, but then will reward something completely different. Embedding these reinforcers into your systems also helps ensure that things are not inadvertently dismantled through casual decisions. Your workforce will see that you mean what you say.

---

[12] "Measure What Matters" by John Doerr and Larry Page

THE CHANGE INSURGENTS

Culture is about people. I hope I've done an adequate job thus far of describing all the ways we tapped into the "many" as we invited our entire workforce to participate in the HMS journey. We created an army of people committed to this company and its mission. They were passionate about sustaining the culture we had achieved.

I would be remiss if I didn't also talk about "the few." To engage the many, you need a few people who relentlessly steward the change process in your organization. These people understand the science and principles that drive change. They drive the changes in practices, processes, and policies that are required to reinforce specific culture. They encourage the agility and dexterity your company needs to respond to the constant change we all face today. They coach and they prod. They make people uncomfortable with the status quo. They drive change through others with unwavering focus.

Back in 2000, Robert B. Reich published a great article in Fast Company that describes this role better than I ever could. The article, called "Your Job is Change" describes the role of the Change Insurgent in an organization and discusses the importance of that role in today's organization. He also outlines the 10 Rules of the Change Insurgent. These rules are not easy. They take real leadership to execute and are essential for radical change. You can find a link to it in the Recommended Reading section of this book.

Tracy South and Deb Kelly were our original internal stewards and change insurgents. They introduced the need for change, advocated for the approach we used, drove our early work, brought Kotter to us, and worked side by side with Kotter, the executive team, and the workforce throughout our journey.

Both Tracy and Deb have backgrounds in Human Resources management; Tracy came with extensive experience leading corporate human resources functions, while Deb's background was in enterprise workforce development and Organizational development. But I have come to believe that finding the right people to play this role in an organization is not based on a role or function. When you choose people from traditional roles—such as HR or OD—you'll sometimes get traditionalists who are more comfortable preventing disruption than driving it. So, you want to look for a set of competencies that provide the unique skillset that enable people to excel in their role as "the few." Here is how I would describe them:

Dot Connecting: The first of these competencies is dot connecting. Dot connectors tend to be abstract thinkers. They can see across a system and find the connections between disparate data points. They can translate complex data into its fundamental simplicity for anyone to understand it. They link everything and help others see connections. Based on my decades of experience, this seems to be a rare skill. So, when you find dot-connectors, do everything you can to engage them.

Low Ego: Your best change insurgents are not attention seekers. They don't want to be CEO or President of the United States. They want to be the wind beneath the wings *of those people*. They want to position others for success and then "sit on the curb and clap" as those they've assisted march by. They don't seek credit; they give credit to others. They generally aren't on stage or in the front row. They are in the back row so they can watch everything and everyone carefully. You must be vigilant not to overlook their contributions.

Truth to Power: The best of these people don't play politics. In fact, this can be detrimental to their success in an organization. They present facts and data clearly. They don't defer to others who might not agree—regardless of the level or power of the dissenters. They don't give up after their first try. They will come back time and time again to make their case. And that case is never about personal gain; their passion is always driven in service to the organization.

Optimism: These people are relentlessly optimistic. They don't allow setbacks to stop them—they use them to reexamine their approach and come up with a new game plan. They believe they can drive change, and they enlist others to believe it as well. They find this work to be fun. Other people want to be in their orbit. You will often find that they lead many more people than are actually assigned to them. Their passion and commitment to change attracts others who will work outside of their day-to-day jobs to become a part of the movement.

Leaders, Not Managers: Many change insurgents will tell you that they consider themselves to be great leaders but lousy managers. Their strength is in creating vision and inspiring others. They have little interest in, or patience for, the management tasks associated with leading a team. They will align themselves with those more skilled at the managerial tasks so that they can focus on what they do best.

Tracy and Deb brought this set of competencies to the organization in the beginning. I didn't know then to look for them. A wise person (my wonderful co-author) once told me that only about 14% of the population has this unique combination of competencies (she even gave me a rock with 14% engraved on it to keep in my pocket as a reminder to be patient with those who think differently).

When Kotter joined us, they brought more of this skillset into our organization. It has been fascinating to watch the evolution of change insurgents blossom at HMS. As we grew, so did the people who made up "the few" who were stewards of this movement. The "few" became a larger team with even more clamoring to be involved. It was organic growth, as people who participated in some of our most impactful initiatives caught the fever and changed careers to help lead our movement into the future.

My advice to you? Find "the few." Nurture them. Free them up to do what they do best. Then listen to them!

A Leadership Legacy

I 've acknowledged that I had come to a place in my career where I was considering my legacy. Yet it was still a shock when my next chapter was thrust upon me a little faster than I had originally planned.

On December 21, 2020, S&P reported:

> "*Veritas Capital-backed Gainwell Technologies announced that it had entered into a definitive agreement to acquire HMS Holdings Corp. at an enterprise value of roughly $3.4 billion.*
>
> *Gainwell will acquire the HMS capabilities focused on the Medicaid market, including for states and managed care organizations, while Cotiviti, another Veritas portfolio company, will acquire capabilities focused on the commercial, Medicare, and federal markets. The transaction is expected to close in the first half of 2021 subject to closing conditions, including HMS shareholder approval and regulatory approvals.*"

With this bittersweet announcement, this chapter of the company I loved—and my role as its leader—would end.

My head and my heart constantly sparred. My head knew this was a positive new step for HMS. It presented an exciting new chapter for the company. By joining forces with two dynamic industry leaders, we would expand our reach, bring together the industry's best talent, provide great opportunities for employees, and ultimately be able to make an even bigger impact on the lives and health of our customers and those they serve. We were acquired at a premium price because of the tremendous value we created for our clients and shareholders through our diverse, inclusive, and passionate culture. It was an acquisition that would serve our customers and shareholders well. Certainly, myself and the HMS workforce had much to be proud of.

Yet, my heart was breaking. I don't have children (though my pets are my kids), but I imagined the HMS acquisition felt like sending your first-born off to college. You've done your job. You've prepared the child for life. And now, you give them flight. Your pride is mixed with sadness and trepidation. You know that things will never be the same, and you wonder if you have done enough to prepare them for what comes next. You know for certain that you will miss your day-to-day interaction with them. And because we sold the company during the COVID 19 pandemic, and I had to say goodbye virtually.

I was leaving the company I had spent nearly half my life building. I was leaving a team I cared for so very deeply—and who cared for me back—and all we'd achieved. Together, we showed that a public company can lead from the head *and* the heart to serve our clients, improve our nation's healthcare system, and deliver shareholder value. Together, we protected our nation's Medicaid program, ensuring the most vulnerable among us could get the care they needed. Together, we returned billions of dollars to our clients to help them cover more people and provide better care. Together, we saved lives by empowering people to take better control of their own health. And together, we showed that we could do it with heart. That's a lot to say goodbye to. No wonder my heart was breaking. My personal goodbye video, the tributes from employees, the emails, and cards, all were overwhelming. I didn't try to hide my joy and grief. I believe being vulnerable makes you more human to everyone in the company. To this day I miss each moment, every funny video I did to get the broader message across, every passionate employee who committed so passionately to our vision. For a while, the feeling of loss was, at times, overwhelming.

Some CEO's or other executives will read this and interpret my message to be that only the soft skills matter; that metrics and KPI's aren't important. That could not be further from the truth. Once employees understand how those KPI's and metrics are designed to monitor the greater good they can have on the world, the result is pure magic.

So, now I ask myself, what did I leave behind? What mark have I made on this company and its people? Ancient Greek statesman Pericles said, "What you leave behind is not what is engraved in stone monuments, but what is woven into the lives of others." I say that "a leader's legacy is established by leaving something of enduring quality behind for the organization and its people." What will be my legacy?

At the beginning of this book, I said that my truest professional legacy is not the company I leave. As proud as I am of that company, I believed that my legacy would be the culture that we created in the company—a culture that engages and empowers the workforce, allows people to stretch, experiment and grow in pursuit of greatness, and which yields results that are almost beyond the imagination. This, I passionately believe, is what will endure in the hearts and minds of those who lived this journey with me.

There is one thing I know to be true. Everyone who joined me on this journey has changed forever. We have learned together that it is possible to create a work environment filled with purpose and passion. We have learned that values are much more than words on a poster—they must be lived in the ways we behave each day. We have learned that giving back—to one another, to our customers, and to the communities where we live and work—makes each of us better. We have learned that every person has a contribution to make—and that they must only be noticed to accomplish astonishing things.

How do I know that the HMS workforce has learned all this? Because they told me. My final goodbyes were virtual as we continued to fight the pandemic. But the outpouring of heartfelt tributes that came from the workforce was heartwarming. What touched me most about the hundreds of messages I received from colleagues is that those tributes focused on the things I care about most—the principles and values I hold most dear. I have selected a few examples to share to illustrate why I am so certain that this amazing workforce will continue my legacy.

Diversity and inclusion (D&I) were always key components of the HMS culture. However, the murder of George Floyd in 2020 was a catalyst to bring our D&I efforts into sharper focus. We took a close look at our organization to determine how we could weave inclusion more tightly into everything we do. With enthusiastic support from our executive leaders, we brought together a broad spectrum of employees to create our first Diversity & Inclusion council. They were a cross-section of our workforce who offered different perspectives influenced by ethnicity, gender, sexual orientation, faith, and abilities. The group quickly went to work on several key initiatives, including:

- Setting up Employee Resource Groups (ERGs)
- Establishing Unconscious Bias training
- Expanding career training and development
- Increasing diversity across senior management
- Strengthening recruiting strategies

Our goals were ambitious but essential. ERGs were formed around several communities (African American, Hispanic, LGBTQ, Veterans and Women) to foster engagement and promote opportunities. Unconscious Bias training became a requisite for employees at every level, leading to better awareness, communication, and collaboration. Career development opened new paths to more diverse representation in management and provided incentives for potential candidates.

Diversity, equity, and inclusion began to thrive at the company, but the work was never ending. We built a solid foundation with passionate individuals to help fulfill our mission of creating a stronger, bolder, more innovative organization. We hired full time staff, including a Head of DE&I, to further reinforce the ongoing commitment to an equitable workplace.

With that said, I had tears in my eyes as I read this very personal note from a courageous young woman in our company:

I talked throughout this book about my belief in diversity and inclusion. I had tears in my eyes as I read this very personal note from a courageous young woman in our company:

> *"HMS hired me almost fresh out of college, and at the time I was a young, scared lesbian—newly out of the closet, struggling with my family and friends. I had no money and nowhere to go, but this company gave me a place where I could carve out a new family and find some stability amidst the chaos in my life. You, Bill, are a big part of the reason I have stayed all these years. I remember early on when my manager told me that you were a gay man, and it made a huge impact on me, that someone of your stature could be out and proud and successful. It made me believe that I could be that way too someday. Through the years I've watched you champion diversity, equality, and integrity. The culture at HMS is unmatched, and we owe that in big part to your example, and all your hard work."*

Another employee shared her story about coming out as a transgender female in 2019. She said:

> *"I authentically worried about how it would affect my life. I embraced my truth and began the process of transitioning. A few months later, you shared to all of us how proud you were of this company, and I truly felt seen. It took everything in me not to cry, as it was powerful to watch. If the world had more people like you serving as leaders, I feel we all would see beauty more often."*

It has always been important to me that every employee felt valued, welcome, and able to contribute. I was proud to see that those who came to us from acquired companies felt it:

> "I find it odd I that feel comfortable to call you Bill and not Mr. Lucia, but that is who you are. I need to thank you, from the bottom of my heart. You made HMS feel like home. I have been so happy this past year being a part of HMS. I have been proud to say that I work for HMS and we do good things for healthcare. You made it that way. You engaged us, welcomed us, made us feel like a part of something huge. You made me feel like part of something important and worthwhile."

> "I haven't been with HMS for long, but I've been here long enough to know that HMS is what it is because of your leadership. I am very aware that the culture of any organization comes directly from its leadership. I quickly realized that HMS was a different kind of company—one that puts its values and heart up front and asks, encourages, pushes, and supports all of us to be the best we can be."

As I write these messages into the pages of this book, tears spring to my eyes, and joy fills my heart. Joy that I was able to steward our cultural journey, which will have a rippling effect for many years to come—and which will benefit all the companies these employees work with throughout their careers. I strove to create a culture that allowed every employee to work with purpose, grow and develop, and come to work every day because they *wanted* to—not just because they *had* to! I firmly believe that work should be more than just a means to a paycheck. Their comments told me that many of my colleagues felt this way too:

> "I wanted to make sure I personally reached out to thank you for being the heart of HMS and showing what it truly means to love what you do. Over the years you have held me accountable and helped develop me into a better leader.

How many employees at a company normally can say their CEO helped them develop and was a model of how to lead and be true to your personality and skills?"

"I've been working in the technology field since 1985 and had long ago given up on finding a larger sense of purpose beyond my job (outside of good relationships with my peers). Thanks to your leadership and the Volunteer Army, that all changed with HMS."

"Thank you for being a once-in-a-career executive who encourages your employees to be our best selves, regardless of job position. Thank you, as well, for reaching out to me when my parents both died from COVID-19 on the same day last summer. That gesture meant a lot to me at a very difficult time."

"You smashed my perception of a CEO/President of a company by being a real person just like us!"

"I cannot begin to thank you enough for all the opportunities you have made possible for me. I have grown so much at HMS and learned what it is like to work for a company that truly values their employees and is so passionate about the work we do—and that is because of you. You are the best leader I have ever come across, and you motivate us all to do better. When you think of all the lives you have changed, please count me among them as I have benefited so greatly by working for you."

I believe in leading from the heart and was gratified to learn how visible this was to the HMS workforce:

"I'm going to really miss having you lead our company. It's not every day a CEO comes along who is so engaged with every aspect of the company and the people and does so with such passion. I've always loved to brag about working for a

company that has a true leader with a big heart who makes us feel like family. That is a rarity! And you are a treasure!"

"You represent everything a leader should be. You lead with your heart, and it always shows. You walk the walk and do exactly what you say. When I describe you to others, I proudly say: genuine, kind, innovative, inclusive, one-of-a-kind, brilliant, and trustworthy."

Finally, and most importantly, I wanted to build a culture that could be sustained beyond my tenure. I wanted to give our workforce the tools, skills, and confidence to understand that they have the power to create a joyful, high-performance work environment where they can serve their customers, their communities, and one another well while they also make a real difference to society. Their comments make me believe that they have learned these lessons well and are as committed to this culture as I was:

"The work environment and culture you helped build is something I've been blessed to be a part of, and as we enter the next evolution of this organization, I think I speak for everyone when I say that we are going to do everything we can to maintain it!"

"You have molded an HMS Army of leaders that have and will continue your legacy wherever they are simply by having had the opportunity to watch you inspire, motivate, and engage everyone around you."

As I reread these quotes from employees, it deepens my conviction that leading from the head AND the heart works. These employees and thousands just like them will always remember their journey at HMS.

And so, I am at peace as I look back on my career. My journey has been more than a dream come true. I never could have imagined that the son of a Philadelphia factory worker and a mom who cleaned doctors' offices would one day lead a successful, publicly traded healthcare technology company. I never envisioned (or even sought) the financial success I have attained. Those are blessings for which I am grateful, but as I close this chapter and look forward to the future, I know those are not the things I'm most proud of. I am most proud of the difference I made in the lives and hearts of people. That will be my lasting legacy.

In fact, today I am advising start-up health tech companies, mentoring entrepreneurial first-time CEOs and continuing my relationships with some of the leaders across HMS – many of whom have leveraged what they learned and moved on to expanded careers. I am now paying it forward and mentoring others – because I love inspiring leaders to be all they can be.

 My advice then, to all aspiring leaders, is this: Culture matters. Leadership matters. Organizational Culture is far too important to leave to chance. Take decisive action to build purposeful culture that engages and empowers your workforce to achieve unimaginable results. Don't fall into the trap of believing that business success requires you to leave emotion at the door. Feel, share your feelings, and show your vulnerability. Be authentic. Be accessible. Don't believe that putting customers at the center of everything you do means forgetting about the employees who serve those customers. Care for your workforce and the environment you create for them first—then let them take care of the customers. It works every time. Culture trumps strategy, but the two together are an unstoppable recipe for success. Define the behaviors required to drive the culture you want and be resolute in living those behaviors. Reinforce them at every turn and don't tolerate those who will not live them. Pay attention to the spiritual and emotional health of your organization and your executive team. Know your people. Communicate in varied and creative ways. Sponsor fun. Good work is joyful. Make sure people know their own value and the value of the service they provide. Give back.

Simply, use your head—and your heart!

Afterword by Cora M. Tellez

When Bill Lucia announced a cultural initiative to transform HMS through the Kotter process, I tried hard to fight the skepticism that came from having personally initiated several company-wide programs designed to engage employees. I've been involved in at least four such initiatives during my 30-plus year career in health insurance, and I have the scars to prove it.

I was happy to be proven wrong. In this book, you've learned the remarkable story of an exceptional leader, Bill Lucia, who began a transformative cultural journey in 2012, shaped the culture of a workforce totaling 3200 employees, and positively impacted the financial and business results of HMS, a Fortune 100 company. As the company's lead independent director, I had a ringside seat to observe and participate (in a very small way) in the transformation of HMS.

Don't be deceived by the slimness of this book—it's filled with insights, real-life experiences, and compelling stories about the things we strive to do with culture. To anyone sincerely interested in initiating and sustaining a cultural shift that will improve business performance, this book is a must read.

Warning: it takes courage and commitment to do what Bill and his executive team have done. Bill's methods are backed by deep analytics and an overwhelming passion to elicit meaningful engagement on the part of the company's employees. If you commit to this journey, be prepared for extraordinary results that will surpass your expectations.

Don't believe me? Just ask Bill.

 *Cora M. Tellez served on the HMS Board of Directors since October 2012. Ms. Tellez is the President and Chief Executive Officer of Sterling HSA, an independent health savings accounts administrator which she founded in 2004. Prior to starting Sterling HSA, Ms. Tellez served as President of the health plans division of Health Net, Inc., an insurance provider. She later served as President of Prudential's western health care operations, CEO of Blue Shield of California, Bay Region and Regional Manager for Kaiser Permanente of Hawaii. Ms. Tellez also served until 2018 as Chief Executive Officer of Amazing CARE Network, Inc., a company she founded in January 2015 (now a part of Sterling HSA).*

Acknowledgements

I've been blessed to have many people in my life who positively influenced my life and career. While writing this book and contemplating the rich career I led, my connection to those people came flooding back. I would like to take the time now to acknowledge some of them.

First, of course, is my family. They shaped me into the person I am today and taught me the values that helped drive my success. While many are alive only in my memories, I am lucky to still have my father at age 96, with his unwavering support. My niece, Theresa, has been the rock in our family and there whenever I needed a shoulder. My brother Frank once told me "you will never succeed if you work for someone else and don't own your own business". I took that advice and ran HMS as if I was more than the CEO and a shareholder – so thank you for that guidance. It just bolstered my view that a financially successful company – public or private can make a major difference in the lives of others.

It has been my great privilege to work under the direction of an accomplished board of directors, who demanded much but supported me always. I would especially like to acknowledge Craig Callen, Ellen Rudnick, Bart Schwartz, Rick Stowe, and Cora Tellez for their guidance, insights, and wisdom during good times and bad. All the directors who served on our board, past and present, deserve a big round of applause and gratitude. You each made a significant difference in our journey and my leadership at HMS. You believed in our journey, the company, and our mission. You brought the right talent to the table at the right time.

I'd also like to thank Bill Miller, whom we sadly lost last year. As former CEO of HMS, he never told me how to get it done; he gave me the freedom to take on big challenges. And my predecessor, Bob Holster, who believed in me for who I was and what I was capable of accomplishing. He also taught me patience—or tried to! Bob was the steady hand when I had to shake things up, focus on culture and drive to our true potential.

I have had the honor of working with the best executive team in the business. Each brought a set of skills that complimented mine and one another's, and each shared my commitment for what this company could be. We made it happen together. Near the end of the journey, Doug Williams, Tracy South, Emmet O'Gara, Jeff Sherman, Maria Perrin, David Alexander, Meredith Bjorck, and Jacob Sims—we did it together! Cynthia Nustad and Semone Neuman, you helped set us on the path to get here and I will always cherish your contributions. There is a long list of HMS employees who helped us build this amazing company; people like Steve Vaccaro, Christina Dragonetti, Donna Price, Michele Carpenter, Ron Singh, Joe Joy. The list goes on.

Special shout-outs to Tracy South for working with me to kick off this journey and shepherding us all along the way, and Doug Williams for embracing this journey so wholeheartedly and expertly tackling some of the hardest projects. I watched each member of the executive team embrace the journey and grow along the way.

No one can get where I got without a lot of support and help from smart friends, and I have had a lot of help. First, I want to acknowledge those people in the organization who supported me. Vern Maczuzak—my chief-of-staff, my hammer, my detail guy—you kept us on track and brought the insights and discipline we desperately needed. Tracie Carter and Melissa Lorenz, without the two of you I would likely be wandering around an airport somewhere wondering where to go next. Deb Kelly—my coauthor, my change insurgent, my "sister from another mister"—you spoke truth to power. You drove change, and you *never* stopped believing in this organization and its people. And I still quote you: "How hard can it be?"

I grew so much from my external "smart friends." Debjani Biswas, you were always by my side, challenging me, teaching me, prodding me, and making me better at what I do. You made me ask myself "If not you, who?" and "What else might be true?"

I know the fearless women in my life have made some of the greatest impact on who I have become.

Dr. John Kotter, David Carder, Jimmy Leppert, Rachel Rosenfeld, and so many supporting players from Kotter—you left us all forever changed. We can never thank you enough for sharing your wisdom, teaching us to apply your principles, and helping us unleash the power of our workforce. You didn't do this to us; you did it with us—and then you prepared us to do it on our own. That is a rare quality in an external partner, and I will always be grateful for the significance of the role you played in our company.

I have always believed in the power of diversity, and this journey provides more irrefutable proof about what can be accomplished when diverse people come together and share ideas, perspectives, and commitment to a cause. I feel so strongly about this that a portion of the proceeds from this book will be donated to Christo Rey (https://cristoreydallas.org/) to help ensure that we continue to prepare a pipeline of diverse leaders to guide the corporations of tomorrow.

Finally, to the HMS workforce. I may have had the amazing honor of leading this company, but you made it what it became. It was a joy each day to watch you serve our customers and those they serve with passion, commitment, and heart. You made a genuine contribution to the health care system, and I will cherish my memories of each one of you. I miss you all each and every day and pray that you use the skills you learned at HMS to make the world a better place.

To all of those at HMS, past and present, this book is my gift to you. My heartfelt thanks.

Sample CEO Blogs

Regular communication with our workforce has played a critical role in creating the high-performance culture I have been privileged to lead. Our workforce craved a connection with me, and I with them. Our core values and messages needed to be continually reinforced. My blogs were one important means of staying in touch with the HMS family. My goal in each was to connect, be real, and speak from my heart. Below are several examples.

REMEMBERING 9/11

 September 11, 2001 seemed like a normal morning. I was on vacation away from my home in Manhattan. I woke up and turned on the television. What I saw would stay with me forever, and I know it will stay with you and all other Americans.

I witnessed the stunned faces of the news broadcasters and saw the second tower of the World Trade Center collapse. I could only imagine the horror and sheer panic of my fellow HMSers, some of whom were watching the tragedy unfold from the roof of our headquarters, which at the time were in Manhattan.

Who could have ever imagined our country as the target of terror? Who could have ever imagined aircrafts flying into two of the tallest skyscrapers in the U.S.? And who could have ever imagined a plane striking the Pentagon? And, if not for the quick action of passengers, a plane most likely would have crashed into the White House.

I've always believed uncertainty to be a terrifying feeling. As a nation, we were very uncertain. Who would be next? Where would the terrorists strike?

Like all of you, I mourned the loss of people and our sense of security. I felt very alone. However, I also quickly felt a new sense of hope. There is no country as resilient as the United States. In the end, the worst would bring out our best.

I remember the bravery of the first responders—including New York's firefighters, paramedics, and police, many of whom sacrificed their lives to save others. I also witnessed the love and humanity in people helping total strangers.

Our HMS family remains committed to remembering the victims of 9/11 through our work in supporting the World Trade Center (WTC) Health Program. The program provides security to first responders and survivors of the attack. I'm incredibly proud of the work we do to ensure the viability of the fund. First responders and survivors will always get the healthcare they need.

Let's remember 9/11 with a sense of hope. We live in a deeply divided country, especially as we move into elections. We need to remember that we are all in this together. We survived 9/11 and prevailed— the same way we have so many times before when our nation was tested. And we will do so again.

STANDING UP FOR JUSTICE AND EQUALITY

I'm writing at a dark time for our nation. We've all seen the horrific video of George Floyd pleading for his life. We share the pain felt by the African American community after another all too familiar tragedy.

Martin Luther King Jr. once said, "The ultimate tragedy is not the oppression and cruelty by the bad people but the silence over that by the good people." We must all speak up and root out hate in all its ugly forms. There's no place in our communities or workplaces for discrimination, racism, or hate. At the same time, I'm sure Dr. King would call for peaceful protest absent the violence we've seen this weekend.

Whether you're a person of color, a member of the LGBTQ community, or any other minority, you deserve nothing less than equality, fairness, and justice. Those are the values we share as a nation.

At HMS, we lead with our values to make healthcare work better for everyone. We do this by leading with both our heads and our hearts to ensure our nation's healthcare system continues to serve the most vulnerable among us.

As your leader, my commitment to you is that HMSers will always support each other and lend our voices and talents to be part of the solution in our communities. This means speaking up for those who have been marginalized for far too long.

As Minneapolis and our entire nation continue to grieve, let's pray justice is served and that we have the courage to make real change. Together, we must build an equitable and just society where all individuals can thrive. Only then will we heal and create a more inclusive world.

BODY, MIND, SPIRIT

I still vividly remember the day my mom passed away from cancer six years ago. She was surrounded by her family. Her husband of 70 years held her hand, stroked her hair, and gently kissed her cheek. Mom suffered from a stroke that took her body but couldn't touch her soul.

Today, there are families across our nation saying goodbye to loved ones dying from COVID-19 via FaceTime and Zoom. Imagine the grief and sorrow of having to say goodbye to your loved one through an iPad.

Throughout this pandemic, our nurses and healthcare workers have become like family members—they provide the comfort we so desperately want to give ourselves. I remember reading a story about a nurse who stayed at the bedside of a patient and held up a phone with the family on FaceTime. The family asked her to brush their mother's hair and hold her hand so she wouldn't be alone as she passed. It's heartbreaking.

As we begin to open up our country, we can't lose sight of how quickly this virus spreads. There are still so many Americans, especially the elderly, who are vulnerable. I haven't seen my 93-year-old father in two months. And I won't see him *because* I love him. At a time when our aging parents need us the most, we can't be with them. Many of you are in this same situation.

This is just one reason why our nation must focus on our mental health as much as physical health. COVID-19 has taught us all how to cope with a situation we've never experienced during our lifetime. The way we live, work, and play has changed. It's okay to talk about our fears, stress, and anxiety—it's perfectly normal and human. We all grieve the loss of nearly 90,000 Americans, a death toll that only continues to rise. If you need to talk with someone, our Employee Assistance Program (EAP) is available to every employee.

Now more than ever, we must take a holistic approach to how we deal with health in our country. To thrive in our new normal, it will take the entire healthcare community, our governments, and citizens to act with both their heads and hearts to take care of our own.

We can all do our part right now. No act of kindness is too small. I would love to hear your ideas or examples of how you're showing concern for others—family members, friends, neighbors, or even strangers you've never met. Imagine the power of sharing ideas and then acting on them.

Please post your act of kindness in the comments section. I'd love to hear from you.

I'm proud of what you do for each other, our clients, and the communities in which we live and work. You lead with your heart and your head—that's what makes HMSers so special.

IT'S PERSONAL: HOW HMS COULD HAVE SAVED MY SISTER'S LIFE

 I want to share a story close to my heart. When I turned 62 in November, it was a difficult birthday for me. I'm now the same age my sister Janis had been when she died of cancer.

At that time, she called me and asked me to talk to our parents. Doing this for Janis was one of the hardest things I've ever done—explaining to my parents that their daughter, their first born, would not survive them.

By the time Janis' cancer was diagnosed, it had spread to her lungs, brain and bones. There was no hope for treatment to save her life. But my sister hung on to her faith, which led to her decision to fight on behalf of her children and grandchildren. Against the advice of her little brother "Billy" and the oncologist, she chose to receive chemotherapy. As a result, Janis was unconscious within three days and passed away two weeks after treatment.

After listening to Annemarie Hull's story about her sister, it reminded me that had Janis' health plan used Elli or Eliza this would not have happened. She never received outreach from her health plan, even though she had very good labor union coverage with Blue Cross Blue Shield. Janis was a smoker and had some illnesses over the years. Clearly, Elli would have identified her as a rising-risk member.

I think back on the pain my parents endured, the great loss we all experienced, and my sister's call telling me about her cancer and saying, "I'm sorry, Billy." I asked her why and she said, "Because I didn't act earlier." An outreach from Eliza would have helped her to act sooner.

Rest in peace my dear sister.

If you ever want to know if HMS' work matters, please think of Janis.

What's your story?

COUNTER RISING FEAR WITH RISING COMPASSION

I'm sure we can all agree: the coronavirus and its rapid spread are scary. I'll admit—I'm a bit scared, too. I worry about the health of our employees, our clients, and the members they serve. Many of those members are elderly, have compromised immune systems, or need more help due to their economic situation.

At the same time, I'm hopeful and inspired by the humanity and determination we see—especially from the doctors, nurses, and community health workers who are on the front lines fighting a global pandemic. No matter who we are, our human nature is to help others—it's in our DNA as a nation and a company.

Think About How You Can Help

We can all help combat the spread by taking steps to protect our own health. Wash your hands regularly and vigorously, avoid touching your face, and stay away from anyone who is sick. Also, remember to practice social distancing. As an Italian, I come from a long line of huggers. But I'm doing my best to avoid hugging *anyone* right now! I try to keep six feet between myself and anyone else. It's not easy, and I admit that sometimes I forget. But if we all do our best to practice social distancing, we can slow the rate of infection.

If you know someone at a higher risk of developing an acute illness from COVID-19, call them regularly to check in with them. For example, my dad is a healthy 93-year-old. But I know his health could change quickly if he becomes infected, so I check in with him every day. And I had a small win—I convinced him to not take the bus to the casino. My dad loves the slot machines!

Reach Out to Those Who Need Help

Let's also keep in mind the families depending on school lunch programs, the elderly and homebound who rely on programs like Meals on Wheels, and others who need help right now. Some may even be worried about being able to feed their pets. With schools closed, some families will find it hard to put food on the table. Organizations that deliver food to homes may be facing shortfalls of food and people to help. I encourage you to reach out to community service organizations and provide donations to help them continue service.

As the world battles this pandemic, it's important to remember the Dalai Lama's words about compassion:

"There are two kinds of compassion. The first comes from a natural concern for friends and family who are close to us. This has limited range but can be the seed for something bigger. We can also learn to extend a genuine concern for others' well-being, whoever they are. That is real compassion."

Events That Will Test Us

Things may get tougher and test our nation, our company, and each of us individually before they get better. However, we will get through this together if we focus on our communities, our friends and families, and our colleagues. I'd love to know what you're doing differently to take care of your communities and those you love. Do you have any thoughts or ideas about what we can do for each other? As always, I welcome your feedback. Just post your comments below.

UNLEASHING HMS' SECRET WEAPON

It's now the fifth month of working from home, our new normal. During this unprecedented time, you continue to display a resilience that leaves me inspired and proud to be leading HMS.

If this experience teaches us one thing, it's how each of us wants and needs to connect with something larger than ourselves. I believe that's why our Volunteer Army continues to thrive and play a significant role in driving HMS' business.

Let me share a few powerful examples of how our Volunteer Army impacts our clients, our brand, and our business ... then consider how this incredible resource could be applied to help you and your teams drive business results.

Helping Our Clients

One of our clients—North Carolina State Health Plan—asked HMS to help boost its subrogation recoveries. The plan covers more than 720,000 teachers, state employees, and retirees. Like many health plans, they too are trying to weather the financial crisis and are looking for ways to save money. We knew we could tap into one of legacy Accent's vendors and use their property/casualty database to find new opportunities for recoveries. However, that's a very time-consuming, people-intensive task. Enter the Volunteer Army. For six weeks, we rotated a group of 12 volunteers who worked for three hours per week. The results were amazing. The Army identified 400 new cases with potential client revenue totaling $3.8 million. Mission accomplished!

Raising HMS' Brand Profile

Building HMS' brand is one of the most important investments we can make in our business. It starts with 3,100 HMSers serving as brand ambassadors. I believe social media is a great equalizer when it comes to taking on much larger competitors. Let me give you an example. When we launched our new Population Health Management campaign, the video we posted to LinkedIn received 400 views. When we asked our Volunteer Army to help amplify our voice in the marketplace, they responded. We now have more than 2,000 views and counting. Mission accomplished!

TBO Boot Camp for New Joiners

The lifeblood of our Volunteer Army is recruiting new members. And who better to speak with HMS' new hires about the benefits of engaging in TBO than our passionate volunteers.

We now have 35 volunteers who host and facilitate TBO Boot Camps twice per month. The goal is to immerse our curious new colleagues in all things TBO. Our volunteers give personal testimonials on how joining the Volunteer Army helped them develop and grow their careers. During these interactive sessions, new joiners get to ask questions and dive deeper into what it's like to step outside their comfort zone and support other areas of HMS' business. Mission accomplished!

If you're not using the Volunteer Army to help drive our business results, then I strongly encourage you to do so. Many department managers have not pursued TBO initiatives with the Army. They are ready and waiting. Please share how you plan to use our Army in the comment section below.

Unleash the Army!

HONORING THE WOMEN OF HMS

Strong. Smart. Fierce. These three words perfectly describe the women of HMS. As we celebrate International Women's Day (IWD), I want to take this opportunity to honor our women and share why I'm so proud of their accomplishments.

This year's theme—"An equal world is an enabled world"—reminds us all that we must take action for equality and break down barriers that women encounter. While much work remains to help forge a gender equal world, I'm proud of the steps our company is taking to ensure women advance and thrive. And I know the men of HMS are also actively engaged in supporting women's equality.

Today, 50% of all HMS leaders are women. The Lead Independent Director on HMS' board of directors is a woman (Cora Tellez). And our Chief Legal Officer (Meredith Bjorck), Chief Strategy and Growth Officer (Maria Perrin), and Chief Administrative Officer (Tracy South), my direct reports, are powerful women who drive our business and serve as role models to both women and men at HMS.

I'm equally proud of our Women's Opportunity Network (WON). Founded by Millie Manning in 2018, WON continues to pave the way in helping women and men further strengthen their business acumen, leadership skills, and technical expertise. From launching a successful mentoring program to leading monthly development programs and personal branding sessions, WON and its 250 members represent HMS on its best day. I'm incredibly proud of the amazing work they do to help other women succeed.

I'm also proud of the work HMSers are doing to help young girls through Girlstart, an HMS Cares partner. Girlstart's mission is to increase girls' interest and engagement in STEM (science, technology, engineering, mathematics) through innovative education programs. Last year, HMS donated $15,000 to Girlstart,and our volunteers showed up in force to help throughout the year.

Salena Torres, a leader in COB Operations, serves as HMS' champion and spearheads our efforts in collaboration with Chief Technology Officer Jacob Sims. The first in her family to attend college, Salena holds a bachelor's degree in chemical engineering and a master's in engineering management. Salena puts her passion to work every day, especially in minority communities, to show the next generation of young women what's possible.

If you'd like to help, HMS is currently partnering with Girlstart for its national "Send a Girl to Camp" campaign, which kicks off on March 14. Visit the site to find out how to support sending girls to

STEM-based summer camps. HMS will match employee donations up to $2,500.

We still have so much work to do. Despite being more than half the population, women still lag in their representation on corporate boards and company management teams, and they earn less than men. As the CEO of HMS, I am committed to creating a culture of equality—where every woman can succeed and thrive.

Strong. Smart. Fierce.

YOU'VE GOT THIS!

 If you're like me, it's getting hard to remember what life was like before COVID-19 and sheltering in place. Our personal and work lives have changed, becoming more intermingled than ever. Many of you have added "homeschool teacher" to your LinkedIn profile and reimagined your home office in clever ways. Whether it's using your ironing board as a standing desk or taking calls from your SUV office, I've seen innovation in action—and I love it!

It's unlikely we'll return to our HMS offices before June, so I want to take a moment to share my thoughts on staying productive to support HMS, your families and our communities during this unprecedented time.

HMS' First Responders

I talk a lot about being agile and putting our clients at the center of everything we do. One great example is the work our Population Health Management team is doing to respond to COVID-19. Through our Eliza solution, we've reached out to 6 million people, ensuring our clients' members receive critical information about the virus.

From helping them learn how to stay healthy at home to providing instructions on how to order vital medications by mail, our Danvers team is working nonstop in the fight against coronavirus. They are HMS' first responders, helping to save lives.

Caring For Our Families

The best part of my day is watching your homemade videos. HMSers have welcomed us into their homes, giving us all a wonderful glimpse into their lives. These videos unite us all because they show our humanity and the day-to-day struggles we all share. Whether you are sheltering in place with children, friends, spouses, partners, parents or pets, life can be messy. Your sense of humor and ingenuity always shine through, so please keep those videos coming!

Paying It Forward

Showing up for our communities has never been more important. In addition to supporting our HMS Cares partners, there are things you can do to give back to others and show small acts of kindness. Think about buying lunch for an essential worker, starting a mask-sewing group in your neighborhood, or watching out for an elderly neighbor by delivering that ever-elusive package of toilet paper to his or her front door. I support small, local restaurants that are still doing takeout or delivery. Small businesses have been hit so hard. Bring moments of joy to others and boost your well-being in the process.

Tell Me What You Yhink

As the coronavirus situation continues to unfold, I'm curious how you think life will change when we return to the office. What do you think you'll do differently at work? How have your relationships with your coworkers changed? What can we do better if we ever experience another crisis like this? I'd love to hear your thoughts. Please share them in the comments section. Stay safe and healthy!

HMS CARES

 If you follow my blogs, you know my parents shaped my values and the core beliefs I'm still passionate about to this day.

Growing up in Philadelphia, our family didn't have much money. My mom worked two jobs cleaning doctors' offices, and my dad worked in a textile factory. But my parents were big believers in the importance of giving back. They expected my siblings and I to share our time and talents to causes we cared about.

HMS' Mission

At HMS, I'm proud of the work we do to ensure the most vulnerable in our nation have access to quality healthcare through Medicaid. We must never forget that our work ensures this safety net program is available to those who have the fewest resources. I'm equally proud of the work we do to improve people's health and well-being through our health engagement efforts. In short, we help the healthcare system work better.

Introducing HMS Cares

Our company and its people have a proud history of giving back to communities where we live and work. It's who we are. And it's what we do. Today, I'm excited to introduce our new HMS Cares volunteer and giving program. Moving forward, we are partnering with charities aligned to our mission of making the healthcare system work better and helping people live healthy lives.

Working Together in Our Local Communities

HMS now has 11 company-sponsored nonprofits we support with our time, talents, and corporate funding. Many of them address key social determinants of health like fighting hunger, providing a safe place to live, and disaster relief. We will focus our time and funding on these nonprofits.

As a healthcare technology company, we will also inspire girls' engagement in science, technology, engineering, and math (STEM). Today, only 24% of STEM jobs are held by women—even fewer in computer science and engineering. We can and must do better as a nation. That's why HMS will do its part to help close the gender gap in STEM careers.

How You Can Help

You can put your passion to work for one of our nonprofit partners by using your eight hours of volunteer PTO. I encourage you to visit the HMS Cares SharePoint site. It includes information about each of the charities HMS now supports.

Pablo Picasso once said, "The meaning of life is to find your gift. The purpose of life is to give it away." I believe that when you have a servant's heart, you'll find a way to use your resources and gifts to help others.

Now, it's time to take action. Use your gifts to serve your local communities. I encourage you to get together as teams to support one or more of our HMS Cares partners.

Bibliography

1. "In Praise of Followership" by Robert Kelley
2. "HBR.org: Three Differences Between Managers and Leaders" by Vineet Nayar
3. "Bringing out the Best in People" by Aubrey C. Daniels, PhD
4. "Culture and Performance" by Dr. John Kotter and James L. Heskett
5. "Measure What Matters" by John Doerr and Larry Page

Recommended Readings

"Bringing Out the Best in People"
by Aubrey C. Daniels, PhD

"Culture and Performance"
by Dr. John Kotter
and James L. Heskett

**"SwitchPoints: Culture Change on
the Fast Track to Business Success"**
by Judy Johnson, PhD., Les Dakens,
Peter Edwards, Ned Morse

**"The Alchemy of Growth: Practical Insights
for Building the Enduring Enterprise"**
by Mehrdad Baghai, Steve Coley
and David White.

**"Accelerate: Building Strategic Agility
for a Faster-Moving World"**
by John Kotter

**"That's Not How We Do It Here! A Story
about How Organizations Rise and Fall--
and Can Rise Again"**
by Holger Rathgeber and John Kotter

"A Sense of Urgency"
by John Kotter

"Measure What Matters"
by John Doerr and Larry Page

"Unleashing the Power of Diversity"
by Debjani Muhjerkee Biswas

"Miserably Successful No More"
by Debjani Muhjerkee Biswas

"The Heart of Change"
by John P. Kotter and Dan S. Cohen"

https://www.fastcompany.com/41467/your-job-change

About the Authors

Bill Lucia is the former Chairman, President and Chief Executive Officer of HMS, a leading healthcare analytics and technology company. He served as CEO from 2009 to 2021 and was named Chairman of the Board of Directors in July 2015. HMS was acquired by Gainwell Technologies, a portfolio company of Veritas Capital, in April 2021.

Under Bill's leadership, HMS grew to $673 million in revenue, serving 500 healthcare payers and 50 government agencies in 40-plus states and 31 of the 38 private health insurers in Australia.

Bill and his leadership team transformed HMS into a high-performance culture by empowering its 3,200 people to act with urgency and excellence to tackle healthcare's biggest challenges. By unleashing the entrepreneurial spirit of all HMSers, employee engagement jumped by 20%, revenue increased by 52% and AEBITDA rose by 82% over a six-year period.

Prior to becoming CEO, Bill served as HMS' President and Chief Operating Officer, driving operational excellence and delivering sustainable growth. He is a named inventor on HMS' patent for Elli, an innovative risk intelligence solution. Bill was also the driving force behind HMS Cares, the company's charitable giving and volunteer program.

Before joining HMS in 1996, Bill held various leadership positions in the life insurance industry. He served as Senior Vice President, Operations, Chief Information Officer for Celtic Life Insurance Company, and Senior Vice President, Insurance Operations for North American Company.

A longtime champion of immigrants' rights, Bill serves on the board of the American Business Immigration Coalition. He previously served as co-chairman of the Texas Business Immigration Coalition. Additionally, Bill is the former chairman of the Council for Medicare Integrity and served on the Healthcare Leadership Council, a coalition of CEOs dedicated to making affordable, high-quality care accessible to all Americans.

Bill now spends his "semi-retirement" advising private equity firms, venture capital firms, digital health incubators and founder/CEOs on investing in and operating companies that make a powerful difference in our nation's healthcare system. He is passionate about protecting our nation's safety net healthcare programs so they can impact people for decades to come. He loves mentoring young CEOs, and much to the chagrin of his financial advisor, often does so pro bono. Bill believes their growth and contribution to making a better healthcare system for all is ample compensation.

 Deborah Kelly is a creative and dynamic organizational effectiveness professional with a proven ability to help companies generate strategic business results through effective people practices.

A graduate of Albertus Magnus College in New Haven, Connecticut, she spent most of her career at Aetna Inc., where she drove some of the company's largest and most successful change initiatives. She joined HMS in 2012 to lead their Organizational Effectiveness function, where she played a key role in driving the company's cultural evolution.

CPSIA information can be obtained
at www.ICGtesting.com
Printed in the USA
JSHW080442150223
37715JS00003B/12